MW00897636

SELF-DIRECTED IRA
IN A NUTSHELL

SELF-DIRECTED IRA IN A NUTSHELL

ADAM BERGMAN, ESQ.

Copyright © 2016 Adam Bergman, Esq.
All rights reserved.

ISBN: 1537045598
ISBN 13: 9781537045597
Library of Congress Control Number: 2016913363
CreateSpace Independent Publishing Platform
North Charleston, South Carolina

TABLE OF CONTENTS

INTRODUCTION

I ndividual retirement account ("IRA") is a term that most Americans have some understanding of. They are commonly aware that it is a type of retirement account that was designed by Congress to encourage people to save for retirement. They generally understand that one can contribute a certain amount of income each year to the IRA account for investment. However, for reasons I will document in this book, most do not have a solid understanding of the concept of tax deferral and the fact that retirement funds can be invested in assets other than stocks or mutual funds through what has become known as a self-directed IRA.

So why don't they know this? It's not because the majority of Americans are uneducated, indifferent, or uncurious—they simply have not been told. There are two reasons.

First, this is because the majority of retirement investment advisers don't know either. I was a tax attorney at several of the largest law firms in the country for close to ten years, and I worked with some of the most highly respected senior tax attorneys in practice today. But whenever I mentioned to such people that IRA funds may be invested in real estate, they did not believe me. Indeed, when I showed them that I had worked with a client to use retirement funds to buy commercial real estate property, and that the transaction was perfectly legal from an Internal Revenue Service ("IRS") standpoint, they were shocked. In one case, one of the senior partners took out his smartphone and visited the IRS website to see if such a transaction was allowed. It was, and is. My point was not to embarrass my law firm or its respected tax attorneys, but to demonstrate that even the most sophisticated investors and tax attorneys are unaware of the possibility of making alternative asset investments using retirement funds.

Second, it's not in the financial interests of the traditional institutional investment companies—such as Bank of America, Charles Schwab, or E-Trade—to encourage you to make alternative investments using retirement funds. They make money when you invest in their financial products and keep your money there for a long time, whether through highly profitable trading commissions or by leveraging the power of your savings. They make no money when you use your money to invest in alternative or nontraditional investments such as a plot of land or a private business. They get no commissions as a result. They lose access to your money, too. Why would they inform you, then, that such a strategy was permissible and possibly even preferable depending on the circumstances?

Yet, such nontraditional or alternative retirement asset investments are perfectly legal. The IRS has permitted them since 1974. It says so right on the IRS website.

And the best way to make those investments is through the self-directed IRA.

Today, out of the roughly 49 million Individual Retirement Accounts in the United States, estimates suggest that only 2 percent to 4 percent of them are self-directed. Basically, this means that almost 95 percent of Americans with Individual Retirement Accounts invest their retirement funds only in traditional, equity-type investments such as stocks and mutual funds.

Before you opened this book, you might have believed that such traditional investments were the only and best way to go.

The nontraditional and self-directed retirement market was relatively small and unknown prior to 2008. A small segment of the investment retirement community were early adopters—they had heard about the nontraditional asset option and took advantage of it to buy real estate, precious metals, and so on. Following 2008, that approach began to become more mainstream. The reason was simple—the blow to retirement savings in the stock market collapse demonstrated the importance of diversifying your portfolio and understanding what you invest in.

In the past few years, the movement toward nontraditional investments has picked up steam. I can't tell you how many times a week I get a call asking whether such investments are permissible and how to make them happen. Those calls come from a cross-section of investors, too: old, young, rich, middle class, as well as from those new to investing and others who are professional investors. According to a McKinsey & Company report, *The Mainstreaming of Alternative Investments*, global alternatives reached record levels of $6.5 trillion by the end of 2011, having grown at a five-year rate of over seven times that of traditional asset classes. And according to a variety of respected researchers, including those from the Federal Reserve Board, the IRS, and the National Association of Government Defined Contribution Administrators, even intuitional investors expect to have 28 percent of their portfolios allocated to alternative investments by 2013, up 26 percent from 2010.

That means more and more people are putting more and more of their retirement assets into nontraditional investments.

IS THIS BOOK FOR YOU?

I've written this book for people who want to learn more about the basics of what a self-directed IRA is and how it works without having to read a 500-page book. In 2015, I published an in-depth, detailed 466-page book on the self-directed IRA structure, *The Checkbook IRA—Why You Want It, Why You Need It: A Private Conversation With a Top Retirement Tax Attorney,* which I am very proud of and which has hopefully helped many retirement investors learn more about the self-directed IRA option. However, in addition to having received some really great feedback from many people and clients who bought the book, I got some comments requesting that I write another book on the self-directed IRA structure that was a bit more introductory and less comprehensive. So I have decided to heed their advice, and I hope this book helps introduce many of the important concepts involved in establishing and using a self-directed IRA to make traditional as well as alternative asset investments, such as real estate, with their retirement funds.

On its own, this book will not help you determine what investments to make with your self-directed IRA. It will not help you to become a successful self-directed IRA investor. But it will give you the fundamentals and basic building blocks for understanding how, potentially, the self-directed IRA can help you build your retirement nest egg. It is up to you to do your homework and leverage your knowledge, experience, and insight to make the best decisions in line with your investment ideas.

The self-directed IRA is a golden ticket to retirement investment independence. It offers the kind of investment diversification and security not available with traditional retirement investments. The goal of this book is to help you better understand the basics, the ABCs, of how the self-directed IRA works so you can ultimately decide whether it makes sense for you.

There is a variety of ways to self-direct your own retirement fund investments—via a custodian or through a special purpose limited liability company ("LLC"). This book will tell you everything you need to know about taking charge of your retirement fund investments through a self-directed IRA so you can benefit from the investment, security, and tax advantages available. I will describe the three types of self-directed IRAs: (i) The traditional self-directed IRA, (ii) the custodian-controlled self-directed IRA, and (iii) the checkbook control IRA. The book will also explore the concept of tax deferral, which is really the last best legal tax shelter out there, while clarifying the IRS rules that govern transactions not prohibited for IRA funds so that you can make any investment with peace of mind. I will also explore some basic tips for avoiding potential fraud, which has recently become more pronounced in the retirement investment community.

Most of all, this book will show you that investing retirement funds does not have to be scary—and it is never dull. Notwithstanding what so many financial advisers and planners may tell you about using a self-directed IRA to buy real estate or make other alternative asset investments, the book will show you that making alternative asset investments with a self-directed IRA is in fact quite easy and simple. Basically, so long as you do not buy life insurance or collectibles, or engage in a self-dealing prohibited transaction with your retirement funds, you can do it by simply writing a check or having the funds wired from the IRA custodian.

The ability to unlock a new world of investment opportunities is at your fingertips. This book will provide you a basic overview of how easy it is to do so through the establishment of a self-directed IRA and show you how rewarding that decision can be.

1

How Jen Got Started with a Self-Directed IRA

ONE OF THE most important of those priorities is taking steps today to ensure we will have enough money to live comfortably when we retire. The path to that future is neither complicated nor difficult. Yet, the first step is a doozy because it requires learning something new, and taking action to make things better in the long-term rather than solving the more immediate problems of today.

I've written this book to make that first step and the journey that follows a lot simpler for you. I'm going to tell you how retirement saving works in general, first by describing the various types of Individual Retirement Accounts (IRAs) that you may already have heard of and even be using. Then I'm going to tell you a lot more about a type of IRA you probably haven't encountered before—the self-directed IRA. The difference between the more commonly used approaches and the approach I'm advocating in this book—the self-directed IRA—is that the latter allows you to leverage your own background, knowledge, and passion to grow your retirement savings directly. And the best part is it is actually much easier and cheaper than you think. I my experience, a hands-on capability and heightened personal interest make all the difference in the world. People who have special knowledge or insight in an investment area are more attentive about their money and more motivated to grow it. They take action and stick to a plan because it's fun, and it feels good to have all the power in their hands. Accordingly, the companies I've built, IRA Financial Group and IRA Financial Trust Company, are designed to help you invest money for retirement through retirement savings vehicles that you can establish, manage, and control.

But first, let me tell you about someone who wouldn't appear in one of those commercials I described, but who may seem familiar nevertheless. I consider this person to be very typical of the clients I work with when setting up a self-directed IRA. I call her Jen.

Jen's Story

Today, Jen is a full-time nurse at a local hospital in Indianapolis. She is fifty-eight years old and is married to Mike with two children. Prior to this position, she was a nurse at a different hospital in Indianapolis for twenty-three years. Jen is in relatively good health and, other than a mortgage and some small credit card debt, she and her husband are in a decent financial position. Jen and Mike enjoy cycling, watching movies, and, most recently, watching home improvement TV shows. Their recent fascination with fix-and-flip home improvement shows had got them thinking about looking into potentially getting involved in a real estate investment. Jen and Mike had talked about this for some time, but kept shelving the idea because they only had about $35,000 in personal savings, which was not going to be enough to buy a home in the neighborhoods they were looking at.

Jen was watching TV one evening when a commercial appeared discussing how one can use retirement funds to buy real estate without incurring any tax on the rollover or on the income and gains from the real estate investment through something called a self-directed IRA. Jen immediately grabbed her smartphone and Googled the term *self-directed IRA*. Jen had heard about IRAs, but had never known that she was able to buy real estate with her IRA. It was as if a whole new world was opened up to her. Jen spent some time reading up on the self-directed IRA and some of the rules involved and jotted down the names of a few companies to call the next morning.

At breakfast, Jen told Mike about the commercial and about what she had learned about the self-directed IRA. Mike was really excited, because he knew that Jen had close to $190,000 in retirement funds, including funds from her former employer, which were in an IRA with a traditional financial institution. Even though he only had a small IRA, he felt comfortable that they would be able to use some of those funds to buy a really great investment property to rent or fix and flip.

At lunch, Jen called a number of self-directed IRA companies to learn more about the self-directed IRA. She was amazed that she had never known the IRS allowed people to use IRA funds to buy real estate or make the most of other alternative asset investments. She and Mike were always under the impression that IRA funds could only be invested in equities, such as stocks, mutual funds, or exchange traded funds. Jen received a number of information kits from the self-directed IRA companies about the self-directed IRA, and she and Mike reviewed it over dinner. Jen and Mike couldn't believe how easy it seemed and just didn't understand why their financial planner nor any of their friends never mentioned the term self-directed IRA. Mike thought it would be wise to call John, a fraternity brother of his, who was a tax attorney at a local firm to get his thoughts on the self-directed IRA structure. Mike sent John an e-mail and John immediately responded that Mike should contact him the next day by phone.

Mike gave John a call and, after some small talk, Mike asked John about self-directed IRAs. John mentioned that he actually had a solid understanding of self-directed IRAs because he had helped a number of clients make investments through that process. Mike was thrilled to hear this and asked John if he could help him and Jen out with their self-directed IRA investment. John agreed and asked Mike if he had a few minutes to spare so he could offer some background on the IRA. Mike said yes.

"Individual Retirement Arrangements (IRAs), as defined by the IRS, exist in many forms. You've probably heard of the most common type—the Individual Retirement Account or IRA..."

"They have the same acronym?" Mike asked.

"Yes. But don't let that confuse you. There are around forty-nine million IRAs in existence today. Believe it or not, most of those forty-nine million IRAs could be considered self-directed IRAs."

"Wait," Mike said. "Are you saying that most IRA holders are using their IRAs to invest in real estate, precious metals, tax liens, or private businesses?"

"Unfortunately not," John answered. "Even if it's allowed under IRS rules, they're not doing that. But what I am saying is that the majority of all IRA investments are technically self-directed since the IRA holder is typically the one who determines what type of investments will be made with his or her IRA."

"You mean, the way my wife selects the mutual funds or even stocks that her IRA purchases?"

"Exactly. When your wife, or any IRA holder, decides which investments to make using his or her IRA, that individual is technically self-directing his or her IRA investment. I wish that more people knew, however, that the IRS allows them to do more than simply select mutual funds or stocks to buy when making IRA investments."

"But I'm getting the feeling that not all IRAs, even those that are technically self-directing, would allow me to make real estate investments."

"That's correct. Whether or not an IRA is a self-directed IRA depends on two factors—control and investment opportunities."

"My wife's IRA is through Vanguard, so I bet she doesn't have that much control."

"Correct again. The 'Traditional Financial Institution' self-directed IRA is by far the most popular type of self-directed IRA. Like your wife's, the majority of all IRAs are held at traditional financial institutions, such as Fidelity, Vanguard, Charles Schwab, Bank of America, Merrill Lynch, and so on. Many traditional financial institutions advertise themselves as offering a self-directed IRAs, but what that really means is that you will be limited to purchasing stocks, mutual funds, bonds, and other traditional types of investments that earn the institution commission. In other words, you need the consent of your IRA custodian before making an investment."

"What's an IRA custodian?"

"A custodian, such as the IRA Financial Trust Company, is your IRA trustee. Basically, that's the institution that holds your IRA account. By law, every retirement account must be held at a custodian or trustee. A trustee may be a bank, trust company, credit union, or a large brokerage firm that is licensed by the IRS. IRS regulations require that either a qualified trustee or custodian hold the IRA assets on behalf of the IRA owner."

"Are there some financial custodians that will allow you to invest in areas you want to invest in?"

"Yes. A true self-directed IRA custodian is known as a passive custodian—and a passive custodian allows the IRA holder to engage in nontraditional investments like real estate. What it generally doesn't do is offer investment advice."

"So, just to confirm, the traditional institutions, such as Schwab or Vanguard, will allow you to establish a self-directed IRA, but they will limit you in what you can buy?" Mike asked.

"Yes—in fact a bank or financial institution, such as Schwab, is not required by the IRS to offer its clients the option to purchase all allowable investments, such as real estate. I want to mention an interesting case called *Guy M. Dabney, et ux. v. Commissioner*, TC Memo 2014-108. In the Dabney case, Mr. Dabney tried to establish a self-directed IRA to buy real estate through Charles Schwab, even though they don't allow for the purchase of real estate with retirement funds. The court ruled that an IRA is allowed to hold real estate, but that the IRC does not require an IRA trustee or custodian to give the owner of a self-directed IRA the option to invest IRA funds in any asset that is not prohibited by statute, such as real estate. The court further held that the withdrawal of the IRA funds from Schwab was not considered a tax-free direct rollover," John explained.

"Interesting. So Mr. Dabney basically said he was going to use his IRA with Schwab to buy real estate on his own, without involving Schwab, and still maintain the tax-free status of the transaction?" Mike asked.

"Yes—basically. I think this case is a perfect example of why you want to use a special self-directed IRA custodian, such as the IRA Financial Trust Company, when making alternative asset investments with an IRA. The traditional financial institutions and banks (IRA custodians), such as Charles Schwab, Vanguard, Fidelity, Bank of America, and so forth, don't make money when you invest your IRA funds in alternative asset investments, such as real estate, and as a result, will not permit you to do so. The court was clear in stating that an IRA custodian is not required to provide its IRA clients with the ability to invest in all IRS-permitted investment options, which is the main reason why there are custodians, such as IRA Financial Trust Company, that exist in the marketplace. The case is a good example of what could happen if one attempts to make a self-directed IRA investment without using a self-directed IRA custodian that specifically allows for the intended IRA investment," John contended.

"OK—I got it. If I want to buy real estate or make alternative asset investments using an IRA, I need to use a special IRA custodian that allows for alternative asset investments, like the IRA Financial Trust Company, but I cannot use a traditional bank, such as Bank of America, or a traditional financial institution such as Schwab?" Mike asked.

"Exactly," John responded.

"Can you trust these IRA custodians?" Mike asked.

"Good question. As long as the institution is authorized to establish IRAs and holds the retirement funds at a Federal Deposit Insurance Corporation (FDIC) institution, you have no worries about your money being safe. In fact, the division of banking in the state where the IRA custodian is established generally governs most IRA custodians. In general, most IRA custodians are established in the state of South Dakota because of its low capital requirements and favorable trust rules."

"So, to get this straight," Mike continued, "when you have a self-directed IRA at a traditional financial institution, you're technically able to self-direct your IRA investments. But you're probably limited to investing in the financial products offered by the financial institution."

"That's right," John answered. "For example, a financial institution such as Vanguard or Fidelity will allow you to select the type of investments for your own IRA, but your choices are generally limited to the financial products they offer. In other words, stocks, mutual funds, and bonds. They won't permit you to make alternative asset investments such as real estate, precious metals, private business investments, foreign currency, options, and so on, all of which are allowed by the IRS."

"Why won't they allow me to purchase real estate with my IRA if it's permitted by the IRS?" Mike asked.

"It's just business. Financial institutions are in business to earn profit and generate strong earnings for shareholders. Like any business, they're motivated to enhance the bottom line. So they require IRA holders to invest in financial products they market and sell. That way they can earn a fee or commission and probably gain use of the funds. In fact, they make money by using the funds they have on deposit for their own investment purposes or to hold as financial reserves."

"In other words," Mike responded, "they don't make any money by allowing you to purchase real estate or other alternative asset investments, so it doesn't make any sense to let you do that."

"Exactly. If they could make money when you bought real estate with your IRA funds, they'd probably allow you to do that. But when an IRA holder buys real estate, the parties that benefit from the investment are the seller of the property, the real estate agent, the title insurance company, and the closing attorney. On the other hand, if an IRA holder uses IRA assets to purchase mutual funds or stocks, the financial institution selling you those stocks benefits directly from the investment," said John.

"So," said Mike, "if they let you shift your IRA assets away from financial products that generate their fees and commissions to nontraditional investments such as real estate, that's going to negatively impact the financial institution's bottom line."

"Right," answered John. "It'll reduce the financial institution's profits for sure, and probably put a strain on its financial reserves. So, most traditional financial institutions just don't allow it."

"So tell me about the financial institutions that allow me to make nontraditional investments with my IRA funds."

"OK," John said. "There are two kinds of those, too. Ready?"

CUSTODIAN-CONTROLLED SELF-DIRECTED IRAS WITHOUT CHECKBOOK CONTROL

"Unlike the traditional financial institutions, such as Fidelity, Vanguard, Charles Schwab, or Bank of America, there are a number of financial institutions or IRA custodians that do allow IRA holders to make nontraditional investments with their IRA funds."

"Have I heard of them?"

"Maybe. They include IRA Financial Trust, Equity Trust, and Pensco Trust, for example."

"Sounds sort of familiar. How are they different from the Vanguards?"

"They have a slightly different business model. Unlike a traditional financial institution, which makes the majority of its IRA-related earnings on commissions and fees associated with stocks, mutual funds, bonds, and other equity or debt types of investments, these custodians typically generate profits through annual account valuation fees and transaction fees."

"OK, so they charge you an annual fee or a fee whenever you do something with your money, or both?"

"Exactly. They generally permit you to make alternative asset investments such as real estate."

"I still don't like that word, 'permit,'" Mike laughed. "It's my money, right?"

"It is," John said, "but even in this type of financial institution you still don't have checkbook control. In other words, you need custodian consent to enter into and execute any transaction."

"Sounds like a pain."

"Well, it can be. In fact, like any bureaucratic matter, it can be very inefficient. There are typically long delays between asking for consent and getting approval, and on top of that, there can be high custodian fees associated with the transaction. So, before engaging in an IRA investment, they require you to get the consent of the custodian. You'll need to provide the custodian with the transaction documents for review as part of its transaction review process. And even upon approval, your IRA investment would be made in the name of the custodian for the benefit of ("FBO") the IRA holder's IRA. So, for example, ABC Trust Company FBO Rich Smith IRA. This doesn't give the IRA owner any privacy or limited liability protection."

"Sounding less appealing by the minute."

"And the minutes can count, right, when you're trying to pounce on an opportunity."

"And the fees, too. I don't like the sound of that."

"You shouldn't. It's common for a moderately active investor with $200,000 in assets with a Self-Directed IRA custodian without checkbook control to end up paying from $500 –to $1,200 in aggregate annual fees (including account value fees, transaction fees, and approval letters). I do want to add that there has been a trend with IRA custodians, such as the IRA Financial Trust Company, toward moving to a flat annual fee, irrespective of account value, at around $360 per year, which, I would think, would make the custodian-controlled self-directed IRA option more attractive."

"And they can still say no to your investment idea?"

"They sure can. There's no guarantee that the custodian will approve your investment even though the investment would not violate IRS rules. Overall, with a custodian-controlled self-directed IRA, even though you will generally be permitted to make most alternative asset IRA investments, time delays and high custodian fees are a major downside. For example, if Jim, the guy who sits in the front row of class, wants to use his retirement funds to invest in real estate, let's say he elects to use a custodian-controlled self-directed IRA to make the investment. He selects ABC Trust Company as the IRA custodian. Before making the real estate investment, Jim would be required to provide all real estate transaction documents, including the purchase agreement and all ancillary purchase documents, to ABC Trust Company for review and signature. Then ABC Trust Company must approve the transaction. If the transaction is approved, Jim needs to wait for ABC Trust Company to sign all documents before proceeding with the real estate purchase. In other words, even before Jim makes an offer on a piece of real estate, he's required to seek ABC Trust Company's consent as well as receive all required signatures before the offer can be submitted. Then, the funds required to make the purchase would be transferred directly from ABC Trust Company, and Jim would be required to pay an annual account fee based on the annual value of his IRA as well as fees for each IRA transaction."

"So, for Jim to pull that real estate deal off, he's got to hope no one else snaps it up before him, ABC Trust Company has to make the purchase for him, and he's got to pay them fees on top of all the fees and costs to the transaction?"

"That's correct."

"I'm assuming there's a better way."

"You're right, there is."

THE SELF-DIRECTED IRA LLC WITH CHECKBOOK CONTROL

John asked Mike if he was good on time, and Mike responded that he had a few more minutes today. John continued.

"Beginning in the mid-1990s, a new type of self-directed IRA structure started taking shape, allowing the IRA holder to make IRA investments directly, without seeking the consent of a custodian. Unlike a custodian-controlled self-directed IRA, which requires the IRA holder to seek the consent of the custodian before making investments, with a self-directed IRA LLC with checkbook control, a limited liability company ("LLC") is established that is owned by the IRA account and managed by the IRA account holder. The IRA holder's IRA funds are then transferred by a passive custodian to the LLC's bank account, providing the IRA holder, as manager of the LLC, with checkbook control over his or her IRA funds."

"So," John added, "with a 'truly' Self-Directed IRA, the IRA holder has total control over his or her IRA funds."

"No need to get custodian consent?"

"Right. You no longer have to get each investment approved by the custodian of the account. Instead, all your investment decisions are made by you, as the manager of the LLC, or by any third-party manager you assign."

John continued. Like the financial institutions and custodians offering custodian-controlled self-directed IRAs, a number of trust companies serve as passive custodians, allowing for true self-directed IRA LLC with "checkbook-control" investments, such as IRA Financial Trust. The popularity of self-directed IRA LLC with checkbook control is increasing each year. More and more custodians are getting more comfortable with their clients using these types of investment structures for their IRA funds.

"What do you think?" John asked.

"I think it sounds great, and I'd love to learn more. Can you teach me what I need to know?"

John said that he could, without much problem. In fact, he'd come prepared to get that ball rolling.

"I have a pamphlet here on the basic rules on IRAs and Roth IRAs in general. I will e-mail it to you. Why don't you read this, or read as much as you'd like, and then we can talk more about the self-directed IRA structure in a few days, after you have gone through the pamphlets I will send you.

"That sounds great," Mike said.

2

The ABCs on the IRA & Roth IRA

MIKE RECEIVED THE pamphlets John sent him by e-mail and started reading about the basics on the IRA and Roth IRAs.

IRAs exist in many forms. The most common type is the traditional IRA, also known as the regular or original IRA, to which any person with earnings from employment may contribute. These types of IRA plans are referred to as contributory IRAs. IRAs that are used to receive assets distributed from other retirement plans are called rollover IRAs. Roth IRAs combine the features of a regular IRA and a savings plan to produce a hybrid that adheres to its own set of rules. SEP and SIMPLE IRAs are technically IRAs, even though their rules are quite similar to those of qualified plans.

An IRA, like the trust under an employer's qualified 401(k) plan, is exempt from taxes pursuant to Internal Revenue Code (IRC) Section 408(e)(i), and an individual maintaining an IRA usually is not taxed on principal or earnings of the account or annuity until they are distributed by the trustee, custodian, or insurance company. A deductible contribution to an IRA thus offers the same tax advantage as an employer's contribution to a qualified plan: deferral of taxation of the contributed funds and investment returns thereon until the funds are withdrawn at retirement.

IRAs can be invested in securities, real estate, or virtually any other asset except life insurance, artworks, precious metals, and other collectibles.

An IRA is subject to some of the prohibited-transaction rules of IRC Section 4975, which imposes excise taxes on self-dealing transactions, and it may be subject to the unrelated business income tax (UBIT) if it invests in a trade or business via a pass-through entity (i.e., LLC) or uses margins or a nonrecourse loan. I will get into these topics later.

THE HISTORY OF THE IRA

In 1974, the Employee Retirement Income Security Act of 1974 (ERISA) was enacted, giving us IRAs. IRAs were created by Congress to encourage savings by employees not covered by qualified plans of their employers.

In doing so, Congress was trying to solve a simple but major problem. For many millions of employees, provision is made for their retirement out of tax-free dollars by their participation in qualified retirement plans.

Unlike a 401(k) and related salary-reduction plans, IRAs are not run by employers. The enactment of IRAs extended to workers without pensions the same kind of tax advantages already granted to pension funds and the self-employed.

Starting in 1975, individuals were allowed to set up separate accounts at financial institutions and deduct the value of their contributions from their current taxable income. To encourage use of the accounts for retirement saving, ERISA set a penalty of 10 percent additional tax on withdrawals by taxpayers before age 59½.

The Economic Growth and Tax Relief Reconciliation Act of 2001 (EGTRRA) increased the maximum allowable contribution to both deductible IRAs and Roth IRAs. For taxpayers under age fifty, the limit would reach $5,000 in 2008 and then would be indexed for inflation. Taxpayers age fifty and above were allowed to make additional contributions up to a limit that would reach $1,000 starting in 2006. In 2016, an individual could make a maximum pretax or after-tax (Roth) IRA contribution of up to $5,500, or $6,500 if over the age of fifty.

While the primary point of the IRA rules is to assist with the gathering of retirement savings, a set of rollover rules is also included, which allows funds to be transferred tax-free from one IRA to another and allows employees to avoid tax on some distributions from qualified plans by contributing the distributed money or property to an IRA.

THE POPULARITY OF THE IRA

According to the Employee Benefits Research Institute, as of 2012, Individual Retirement Accounts (IRAs) are a vital component of US retirement savings, holding more than 25 percent of all retirement assets in the nation. Substantial portions of these IRA assets originated in other tax-qualified retirement plans, such as defined benefit plans (pensions) and 401(k) plans, and were moved to IRAs through rollovers from those plans. Thus, a sizable percentage of current IRA accounts are a repository for assets built up in the employment-based retirement system, as individuals hold money in them before or during retirement.

According to the ICI Research Perspective publication of January 2015, $7.3 trillion in IRA assets existed at the end of the second quarter of 2014. IRAs represented more than one-quarter of total United States retirement-market assets, compared with 17 percent two decades ago. IRAs also have risen in importance on household balance sheets. In mid-2014, 36 percent of households headed by an individual age 45 to 54 owned IRAs, and 37 percent of households headed by an individual age 55 to 64 owned IRAs.

Traditional IRAs were the most common type of IRA owned, followed by Roth IRAs and employer-sponsored IRAs such as SEP IRAs.

WHAT IS AN IRA?

An individual retirement account (IRA) is a trust or custodial account set up in the United States for the exclusive benefit of you or your beneficiaries. The account is created by a written document. The document must show that the account meets each of the following requirements:

• The trustee or custodian must be a bank, a federally insured credit union, a trust company, a savings and loan association, or an entity approved by the IRS to act as trustee or custodian.

- The trustee or custodian generally cannot accept contributions of more than the deductible amount for the year. However, rollover contributions and employer contributions to a simplified employee pension (SEP) can be more than this amount.
- Contributions, except for rollover contributions, must be in cash.
- You must have a nonforfeitable right to the amount at all times.
- Money in your account cannot be used to buy a life insurance policy.
- Assets in your account cannot be combined with other property, except in a common trust fund or common investment fund.
- You must start receiving distributions by April 1 of the year following the year in which you reach age 70½ (required minimum distributions).

There are two kinds of IRAs: individual retirement accounts (trusts and custodial) and annuities (contracts).

HOW DO I SET UP AN IRA?

An individual may establish an IRA with a bank, savings and loan association, credit union, trust company, brokerage firm, or other organization that can demonstrate to the IRS the ability to lawfully administer the IRA account. The trustee or custodian must be a bank, a federally insured credit union, a savings and loan association, or an entity approved by the IRS to act as trustee or custodian. An individual retirement annuity is generally established through an insurance company.

To establish an IRA, the IRA holder and the financial organization offering the IRA must agree upon certain terms and conditions in writing. An IRA is established when the individual and the financial institution sign and receive the IRA-opening documents. You can set up an IRA at any time. When the IRA is opened, it is essentially a trust with no investments. The IRA is funded when the IRA owner makes contributions or funds are transferred or rolled over from another retirement account.

WHO TENDS TO SET UP IRAS?

IRA owners tend to be savers. According to the ICI Research Perspective publication from November 2013, the median financial assets of IRA-owning households were eight times greater than the median financial assets of households that did not own IRAs. Also, IRA owners are more likely to be married, employed, and have college or postgraduate degrees than households that do not own IRAs.

HOW MANY IRAS CAN I HAVE?

An IRA holder may have an unlimited number of IRAs with one or more financial organizations. So, if you are under fifty years old and have three different IRAs, as of 2016 you cannot make IRA contributions in an amount that will exceed $5,500, including to all of your IRA accounts ($6,500 if you are over the age of fifty). The contribution can be allocated to one IRA or divided among all or some of the other IRA accounts.

Can I Have an IRA if I Also Contribute to Another Retirement Account?

If both you and your spouse have compensation and are under age 70½, each of you can set up an IRA. You can have a traditional IRA whether or not you are covered by any other retirement plan. However, you may not be able to deduct all of your contributions if you or your spouse is covered by an employer-retirement plan.

If you and your spouse file a joint return, only one of you needs to have compensation. You and your spouse cannot both participate in the same IRA.

THE TRADITIONAL IRA

According to the ICI Research Perspective publication of January 2015, about one-quarter of US households owned traditional IRAs in 2014. Traditional IRAs were the most common type of IRA owned, followed by Roth IRAs and employer-sponsored IRAs.

A traditional IRA primarily is a tax-deferred retirement-savings vehicle. Tax is generally deferred on traditional IRA contributions and earnings until the year the IRA owner takes a distribution. A traditional IRA is essentially any IRA that is not a Roth IRA or a SIMPLE IRA. In general, if you have income from working for yourself or someone else, you may establish and contribute to an IRA. The IRA can be a special account that you set up with a bank, brokerage firm, or other institutional custodian. Alternatively, it can be an individual retirement annuity you purchase from an insurance company.

WHO CAN SET UP A TRADITIONAL IRA?

You can set up and make contributions to a traditional IRA if:

- you (or, if you file a joint return, your spouse) received taxable compensation during the year, and
- you were not age 70½ by the end of the year.

You can generally set up a traditional IRA if you have income from working for yourself or someone else. If your only income is Social Security or passive income, such as interest, dividends, rental income, or capital gains, that income would not be considered earned income and would not be considered income available for purposes of making an IRA contribution.

TAX-DEDUCTIBLE CONTRIBUTIONS

With traditional IRA contributions, you have the ability to take tax deductions. This was designed to encourage saving for retirement.

When you take advantage of tax deferral by investing in your employer-sponsored retirement plan, you not only put off paying income taxes on the money you contribute, you may also save money on the taxes you eventually will pay.

The money you contribute to a traditional IRA is pretax, which means that the contribution is deducted from your gross income and goes directly into your retirement-savings plan, so that you're left with a smaller dollar amount in your paycheck that can be taxed by the IRS. As a result, you'll pay less in your current income taxes for the year because, according to the IRS, you've earned less money. This can help you reduce your income-tax liability.

The benefit of tax-deductible contributions is simple. For example, if you are in a 30 percent income-tax bracket and you contribute $5,000 to a traditional IRA in a year, that's $5,000 of your salary on which you're not paying taxes this year; so, you will be able to reduce your annual income tax bill by approximately $1,500 ($5,000 × 30 percent). In other words, you will receive an income-tax deduction for the $5,000 contribution, which will save you approximately $1,500 in tax payments. By making tax-deductible contributions, you are essentially paying yourself to save for your retirement.

All earnings generated from traditional IRA contributions are tax deferred until distributed.

WHAT IS TAX DEFERRAL?

Tax deferral literally means that you are putting off paying tax. The most common types of tax-deferred investments include those in IRAs or Qualified Retirement Plans (i.e., 401(k) plans). Tax deferral means that all income, gains, and earnings, such as interest, dividends, rental income, royalties, or capital gains, will accumulate tax-free until the investor or IRA owner withdraws the funds and takes possession of them. As long as the funds remain in the retirement account, the funds will grow tax-free. This allows your retirement funds to grow at a much faster pace than if the funds were held personally, allowing you to build for your retirement more quickly. And when you withdraw your IRA funds in the form of a distribution after you retire, you will likely be in a lower tax bracket and be able to keep more of what you have accumulated. So, by using a traditional IRA as a retirement-savings vehicle, not only are you not paying taxes on the money you invested, you could be paying them at a lower rate when you finally do "take home" your money.

As long as the funds remain in the account, they grow without taxes eroding their value. This enables assets to accumulate at a faster rate, giving you an edge when saving for the long term.

"We will spend a considerable amount of time talking about tax deferral the next time we meet, but I just wanted to introduce you to the concept of tax deferral," John said.

What Are the Advantages of Tax Deferral?

By using an IRA to make investments, the IRA owner is able to defer taxes on any investment returns, thus allowing the IRA owner to benefit in three ways. The first benefit is tax-free growth: instead of paying tax on the returns of an investment, tax is paid only at a later date, leaving the investment to grow tax-free without interruption. The second benefit of tax deferral is that IRA investments are usually made when the IRA owner is in his or her highest income-earning years and is thus subject to tax at a higher tax rate. The third benefit is the ability to defer taxes on investments in the face of increased federal income-tax rates. With tax rates at a historic low (the highest income-tax bracket in 1986 was 50 percent; in 2000, it was 39.6 percent), the likelihood of higher federal income-tax rates in the near future is significant, especially with the financial strain the baby-boomer generation is expected to have on the federal budget. Thus, the ability to defer tax on investments until the IRA owner is 70½, and likelier to be in a lower income-tax bracket, makes an IRA a highly attractive investment vehicle.

Tax Deferral by the Numbers

The following examples illustrate the powerful advantage of tax-deferred contributions and compounding through a traditional IRA versus making contributions to a taxable account.

Example 1

Joe is forty years old and makes a $5,000 contribution to an IRA. Assume Joe is in a 30 percent federal income-tax bracket. Joe invests his IRA funds and receives a 6 percent average annual return. When Joe retires at age seventy, his $5,000 contribution would be worth $21,609.71. If Joe had invested the $5,000 personally, the account would only be worth $14,033.97.

Example 2

Jane is thirty-five years old and makes a $5,000 contribution to an IRA. Jane makes a $5,000 contribution to her IRA each year until she reaches the age of seventy. Assume Jane is in a 30 percent federal income-tax bracket. Further, assume that Jane was able to generate a 7 percent average annual return on her investment. When Jane retires at the age of seventy, her IRA account would be worth $792,950.21. If Jane had made these $5,000 contributions though a taxable account, the account would only be worth $490,707.49.

TRADITIONAL IRA CONTRIBUTIONS

IRC Section 219(a) permits a deduction for contributions to IRAs, which is allowable only if the contribution is in cash, the contributor is under the age of 70½ at the end of the taxable year, and the contribution is not a rollover. Also, a deductible contribution may not be made to an IRA that was started by another person and acquired by the taxpayer as beneficiary on that person's death unless the taxpayer is the surviving spouse.

HOW MUCH CAN BE CONTRIBUTED?

Traditional IRAs may receive several types of contributions: regular, spousal, rollover, transfer, recharacterization, and catch-up contributions.

REGULAR CONTRIBUTIONS

To be eligible to make regular contributions to a traditional IRA, an individual must satisfy the age requirements for that year and have earned income.

AGE

There is a maximum-age restriction under the law on when traditional IRA contributions can be made. IRA owners cannot make IRA contributions beginning in the year in which they attain age 70½. Therefore, IRA owners who reach their seventieth birthday before July 1 of a given year cannot make an IRA contribution for that year because they will be 70½ before the end of the year.

There is no minimum age for making IRA contributions; however, financial institutions may have rules restricting minors from signing contracts.

QUALIFIED COMPENSATION
Individuals must have qualified compensation in order to be eligible to contribute to an IRA. In general, individuals must earn income from personal services rendered. The personal services rendered must be performed in the year the compensation is received. For most individuals, the income is shown on IRS Form W-2, Wage and Tax Statement, or IRS Form 1099-MISC.

WHAT IS COMPENSATION?
Generally, compensation is what you earn from working.

- Wages, Salaries, and so on
  Wages, salaries, tips, professional fees, bonuses, and other amounts you receive for providing personal services are compensation.
- Commissions
  An amount you receive that is a percentage of the profits or sale price is compensation.
- Self-Employment Income
  If you are self-employed (a sole proprietor or a partner), compensation is the net earnings from your trade or business (provided your personal services are a material income-producing factor) reduced by the total of
  - the deduction for contributions made on your behalf to retirement plans, and
  - the deduction allowed for one-half of your self-employment taxes.
- Alimony and Separate Maintenance
  For IRA purposes, compensation includes any taxable alimony and separate maintenance payments you receive under a decree of divorce or separate maintenance.
- Military Differential Pay
  For IRA purposes, compensation includes military differential pay you receive.
- Nontaxable Combat Pay
  If you were a member of the US armed forces, compensation includes any nontaxable combat pay you received.

WHAT IS NOT COMPENSATION?

Compensation does not include any of the following items:

- Earnings and profits from property, such as rental income, interest income, and dividend income
- Pension or annuity income
- Deferred compensation received (compensation payments postponed from a past year)
- Income from a partnership for which you do not provide services that are a material income-producing factor
- Any amounts (other than combat pay) you exclude from income, such as foreign-earned income and housing costs
- Income from Social Security and workers' compensation

What IS and is NOT Compensation for Purposes of an IRA

Compensation includes...	Compensation does NOT include...
Wage / Salaries	Earnings and profits from real estate investments
Commissions	Interest and dividend income
Self-employment income	Pension or annuity income
Alimony and separate maintenance	Deferred compensation
Military differential pay	• Income from certain partnerships that does not involve [?] • Any amounts you exclude from income • Income from social security and worker's compensation
Nontaxable combat pay	

WHAT IF BOTH SPOUSES HAVE COMPENSATION?

If both you and your spouse have compensation and are under age 70½, each of you can set up an IRA. You cannot both participate in the same IRA. If you file a joint return, only one of you needs to have compensation for each spouse to open his or her own IRA.

CONTRIBUTION LIMITS

Under the IRA rules, a contribution is deemed to have been made during a taxable year if it is made not later than the due date of that year's return (not including extensions) and is "made on account of such taxable year." For a taxpayer whose taxable year is the calendar year, a contribution for any year can thus be made as late as April 15 of the following year. For example, for 2016, you will be permitted to make IRA contributions up until April 15, 2017.

REGULAR CONTRIBUTIONS

A regular traditional IRA contribution is limited to the lesser of the annual contribution limit or 100 percent of the individual's eligible compensation.

Example 1

If Jim earned $25,000 in W-2 compensation in a year and is under fifty years of age, Jim would be permitted to make a $5,500 IRA contribution in 2016.

Example 2

If Jim earned only $4,000 in W-2 compensation in a year and is under fifty years of age, Jim would only be permitted to make an IRA contribution of $4,000.

For the year 2016, you may contribute a maximum of $5,500 each year, or $6,500 if you will reach the age of fifty by the end of the year. If you are not covered by an employer's retirement plan, you may take a deduction on your tax return for your contribution. However, if you are covered by an employer's plan, your IRA may be fully or partially deductible, or not deductible at all, depending on how much gross income you have.

CATCH-UP CONTRIBUTIONS

Individuals who reach age fifty or older before the end of the taxable year may be eligible to contribute an additional amount to a traditional IRA as a catch-up contribution. The maximum annual amount that individuals may contribute to a traditional IRA as a catch-up contribution is $1,000.

SPOUSAL CONTRIBUTIONS

If an individual has no qualified compensation income but his or her spouse does, that individual may generally make a contribution to his or her IRA based on his or her spouse's compensation. This is generally referred to as "spousal contributions."

To be eligible for spousal contributions to a traditional IRA, the spouse without compensation income must not have reached the age of 70½ in the calendar year in which the contribution is being made. Also, to be eligible, the spouse must have eligible compensation and the couple must file a joint federal income-tax return.

The traditional IRA contribution limits are applied to each spouse as a separate IRA holder. Thus, if both a husband and wife are eligible to make IRA contributions, the IRA contribution limit for the couple in 2016 is the lesser of $11,000 (plus catch-up contributions, if eligible) or 100 percent of the combined eligible compensation. However, no more than the individual IRA individual contribution limit ($5,500, plus catch-up contributions, if eligible) may be contributed to either spouse's IRA.

If a spousal contribution is made, the spouse without compensation must establish a separate IRA. However, the compensated spouse is not required to have an IRA in order for the noncompensated spouse to make an IRA contribution.

Example 1

Jim and Jane are married and both earn $25,000 in W-2 compensation annually. Jim and Jane are both under fifty years of age. Jim and Jane would each be permitted to make a $5,500 yearly IRA contribution for 2016.

Example 2

Jim and Jane are married. Jim and Jane are both under fifty years of age. Jim did not earn any yearly compensation, but Jane earned $50,000 in W-2 annual compensation. Jim would still be able to make a spousal contribution of $5,500 based on Jane's eligible compensation for 2016.

CAN I CONTRIBUTE LESS THAN THE MAXIMUM ALLOWED CONTRIBUTIONS?

You are not required to make maximum contributions to your IRA each year. In fact, you are not required to make any contributions to your IRA in any year. However, if contributions to your traditional IRA for a year are less than the limit, you cannot contribute more after the due date of your return for that year to make up the difference.

Example

Jim, who is forty-seven, earned $47,000 in year 2014. Although he can contribute up to $5,500 for that year, Jim only made a contribution of $3,700. After April 15, 2015, Jim cannot make up the difference between his actual contributions for 2014 ($3,700) and his 2014 limit ($5,500). He cannot contribute $1,800 more than the limit for any later year.

WHAT HAPPENS IF I CONTRIBUTE MORE THAN THE MAXIMUM CONTRIBUTIONS?

If contributions to your IRA for a year are more than the maximum IRA contribution limit, for that year, you can generally apply the excess contribution in one year to a later year if the contributions for that later year are less than the maximum allowed for that year. However, a penalty or additional tax may apply.

In general, if the excess contributions for a year are not withdrawn by the date your return for the year is due (including extensions), you are subject to a 6 percent tax. You must pay the 6 percent tax each year on excess amounts that remain in your traditional IRA at the end of your tax year. The tax cannot be more than 6 percent of the combined value of all your IRAs as of the end of your tax year. (The additional tax is figured on Form 5329.) You will not have to pay the 6 percent tax on an excess IRA contribution if you with-draw an excess contribution made during a tax year, and you also withdraw any interest or other income earned on the excess contribution. You must complete your withdrawal by the date your tax return for that year is due, including extensions.

IF I HAVE A 401(K), CAN I STILL CONTRIBUTE TO AN IRA?

In the past, an active participant in an employer-sponsored retirement plan could not have an IRA. This restriction was removed in 1981, but it reap-peared in modified form in 1986. Since 1986, the normal ceiling on deductible IRA contributions has been reduced if the taxpayer is an "active participant" of a qualified retirement plan and his or her adjusted gross income exceeds a threshold amount. In other words, rather than disqualifying all employees participating in employer-sponsored plans, the IRA deduction is phased out for taxpayers whose incomes exceed specified thresholds.

WHAT IRA CONTRIBUTIONS ARE DEDUCTIBLE?

In general, an IRA owner is able to deduct a traditional IRA contribution, or a portion of an IRA contribution, depending on the IRA owner's active participation in an employer-sponsored retirement plan, such as a 401(k) plan; marital status; and modified adjusted gross income (MAGI).

WHAT IS THE TRADITIONAL IRA DEDUCTIBILITY THRESHOLD FOR 2016?

In 2016, if you are single and covered by an employer's plan, your contribution is fully deductible if your adjusted gross income (AGI) is less than $61,000 and not deductible at all when your AGI reaches $71,000. Between $61,000 and $71,000, the deduction is gradually phased out. For married individuals, the phase-out range is from $98,000 to $118,000, if the IRA participant is covered by an employer plan. For an IRA participant who is not covered by a plan but whose spouse is covered, the phase-out range is $184,000–$194,000.

TRADITIONAL IRA *NONDEDUCTIBLE* CONTRIBUTIONS

An individual who is unable to deduct all or part of a traditional IRA contribution is still permitted to make a nondeductible traditional IRA contribution of up to the lesser of the applicable annual limit (i.e., $5,500 if the individual is under the age of fifty for 2016) or 100 percent of earned income.

An IRA owner who makes a nondeductible traditional IRA contribution must report the nondeductible amount to the IRS on Form 8606, which should be filed with the IRA owner's individual federal income-tax return (Form 1040).

CAN I STILL MAKE IRA CONTRIBUTIONS EVEN IF I EARN MORE MONEY THAN THE PHASE-OUT LIMIT?

A taxpayer phased out of making tax-deductible contributions is still allowed to make nondeductible contributions in the amount of $5,500 or $6,500, as applicable for 2016.

DISTRIBUTIONS

The IRS's approach to helping people invest and save their retirement funds is a lot like a football game. If the quarterback takes too much time calling an offensive play, the team will face a penalty. Similarly, if a traditional IRA owner withdraws his or her funds too early from an IRA, the IRA owner will face an early distribution tax.

The required distribution rules are believed to have been designed by Congress to ensure that IRAs are mainly used as retirement-savings vehicles, not as a medium to build wealth for transfer to heirs.

In general, the distribution rules deal separately for distributions to IRA owners and distributions to beneficiaries after the death of an IRA owner.

WHEN CAN DISTRIBUTIONS BE TAKEN FROM AN IRA?

An IRA owner may take distributions from his or her IRA at any time. The determination of whether the distribution is taxed depends on the type of IRA (i.e., traditional or Roth); the age of the IRA owner; and, in the case of a Roth IRA, the duration of time the account has been established.

ARE TRADITIONAL IRA DISTRIBUTIONS SUBJECT TO TAX?

Yes, the IRA owner is required to include traditional IRA distributions in his or her taxable gross income. The IRA owner who receives a distribution will report the distribution on his or her individual federal income-tax return (Form 1040) and pay tax on the distribution based on the individual's federal income-tax rate.

WHAT TYPE OF TRANSACTIONS ARE EXEMPTED FROM THE TRADITIONAL IRA DISTRIBUTION RULES?

In general, the following IRA-related transactions are not treated as distributions subject to tax:

- rollovers;
- transfers;
- recharacterizations;
- revoked IRA within seven-day period; and
- the portion of a distribution relating to nondeductible traditional IRA contributions.

EARLY DISTRIBUTIONS

In general, traditional IRAs are designed to encourage retirement saving and at the same time discourage people from taking money away from their retirement savings before reaching the age of 59½. The age 59½ was selected by Congress because it was believed to be the age when one began transitioning from active employment to retirement.

ARE EARLY DISTRIBUTIONS SUBJECT TO AN ADDITIONAL TAX?

Yes. In general, the IRS assesses a 10 percent penalty on the taxable portion of early distributions. However, the 10 percent early-distribution penalty does *not* apply in the following situations.

1. **Death of the IRA Owner**
   An IRA distribution to beneficiaries is not subject to the 10 percent early-distribution penalty. In other words, upon the death of the IRA owner, the distribution of the owner's IRA to his or her beneficiaries is not subject to the 10 percent penalty.
2. **Disability**
   Distributions received by a disabled IRA owner are not subject to the 10 percent early-distribution penalty. Prior to making the disability distribution, the financial organization may require written evidence from the disabled IRA owner to verify disability. The IRA owner can demonstrate this by using IRS Form 1040, Schedule R, Credit for the Elderly or Disabled.
3. **Rollovers and Conversions**
   Amounts rolled over to an IRA or properly converted to an IRA are not subject to the 10 percent early-distribution penalty.
4. **First-Time Homebuyer Expenses**
   Distributions taken for qualified first-time homebuyer expenses are not subject to the 10 percent early-distribution penalty. There is a $10,000 lifetime limit with this exemption.

5. **Return of Nondeductible Contributions**

   The 10 percent early-distribution penalty would not apply to the portion of a distribution that represents a return of nondeductible contributions or after-tax assets received through a rollover.

6. **Substantially Equal Periodic Payment**

   The 10 percent early-distribution penalty shall not apply to distributions that are part of a series of substantially equal periodic payments made at least annually over the IRA owner's life expectancy or the joint life expectancy of the IRA owner and his or her beneficiary. The IRA holder must make a specific election under IRC Section 72 with the IRA custodian to take advantage of this election. The rules that apply to this option are quite complex, so it is best to consult with a tax attorney or CPA.

7. **Health Insurance**

   An IRA owner who received federal or state unemployment compensation for twelve consecutive weeks may take IRA distributions to pay for health insurance. These distributions are not subject to the 10 percent early-distribution penalty. The IRA owner must take a distribution in the year he or she received unemployment or in the year that follows. This exemption does not apply to distributions taken more than sixty days after the IRA owner regains employment.

8. **Medical Expenses**

   Distributions used for reimbursed medical expenses that exceed 7.5 percent of the IRA owner's adjusted gross income are not subject to the 10 percent early-distribution penalty.

9. **Higher-Education Expenses**

   IRA distributions used for qualified education expenses of the IRA owner, his or her spouse, or the spouse's child or grandchild are not subject to the 10 percent early-distribution penalty.

10. **IRS Levy**

    Distributions taken because of IRS tax levies imposed on the IRA owner are not subject to the 10 percent early-distribution penalty.

11. **Qualified Reservist Distributions**

Qualified reservists (including National Guard personnel) called to active duty after September 11, 2001, for a period of at least 180 days or an indefinite amount of time, are permitted to take penalty-free distributions from their IRA. This applies to distributions taken between the date of the order or call to duty and the end of the active-duty period. Also, the distribution taken will still be subject to federal income tax.

REQUIRED DISTRIBUTIONS TO IRA OWNERS

The required minimum distribution rules (RMDs) were created in order to guarantee the flow of IRA funds into the federal income-tax system as well as to encourage IRA owners to use their retirement funds during their retirement.

You don't have to be concerned about taking distributions from a retirement plan until the year in which you turn 70½. To avoid penalty, an IRA owner must comply with what are called the required distribution rules, also known as the minimum distribution rules. The required distribution rules require that an IRA owner take a minimum distribution amount from his or her retirement account each year, generally beginning in the year the IRA owner turns 70½. The rules are somewhat extensive, so I don't want to spend much time on this; but it is important to know that once you turn 70½ and have a pretax IRA, you will be required to take into income a small percentage of your entire IRA value each year. A number of free RMB calculators are available online that allow you to plug in your age and total IRA value so that you can identify your annual RMD amount. For example, if you are 75 years old and have a pretax IRA valued at $200,000 as of December 31, in 2016 your RMD amount would be $8,733.62. Interestingly, the RMD rules do not apply to Roth IRAs.

BENEFICIARY DISTRIBUTION OPTIONS

A number of distribution options are available to a designated IRA beneficiary, generally dependent on whether the deceased IRA owner's sole primary beneficiary is a spouse and whether the deceased IRA owner has reached 70½, the age for RMDs. Remember, a living IRA owner is not required to take an RMD until the IRA owner reaches the age of 70½. I don't want to get into too much detail on how beneficiary distributions are made since the calculations are somewhat complex, and the IRA custodian you are using will help you calculate the annual RMD amount.

THE ROTH IRA

The Roth IRA was originally called an "IRA Plus"; the idea was proposed by Senator Bob Packwood of Oregon and Senator William Roth of Delaware in 1989. The Packwood-Roth plan would have allowed individuals to invest up to $2,000 in an account with no immediate tax deductions, but the earnings could later be withdrawn tax-free at retirement.[1]

The Roth IRA was established by the Taxpayer Relief Act of 1997 (Public Law 105-34) and named for its chief legislative sponsor, Senator William Roth of Delaware. When the landmark legislation was passed, Senator Roth and his colleagues did not quite know what they had created and how much of an impact it would ultimately have on Americans and their ability to have a financially secure retirement.

Since 1997, the Roth IRA has not only grown in stature and popularity, but it has become one of the cornerstones of many Americans' retirement portfolios. Originally, American taxpayers were only allowed to contribute up to $2,000 of their after-tax earned income to a Roth IRA, and there was not yet a catch-up contribution allowed for citizens over the age of fifty. It took several years for the contribution limits to increase to the current amounts of $5,500 per taxpayer or $6,500 if one is over fifty years of age and making a catch-up contribution.

The big advantage of a Roth IRA is that, if you qualify to make contributions, all distributions from the Roth IRA are tax-free—even the investment returns—as long as the distributions meet certain requirements. In addition, unlike traditional IRAs, you may contribute to a Roth IRA for as long as you continue to have earned income (in the case of a traditional IRA, you can't

---

1. https://en.wikipedia.org/wiki/Roth_IRA.

make contributions after you reach age 70½). The rules for the Roth IRA are found in the IRC under Section 408A.

WHAT IS A ROTH IRA?

A Roth IRA is an IRA that the owner designates as a Roth IRA. A Roth IRA is generally subject to the rules for traditional IRAs. For example, traditional and Roth IRAs and their owners are identically affected by the rules treating an IRA as distributing its assets if the IRA engages in a prohibited transaction or the owner borrows against it. The reporting requirements for IRAs also apply to Roth IRAs. However, several rules, described below, apply uniquely to Roth IRAs.

The most attractive feature of the Roth IRA is that, even though contributions are not deductible, all distributions, including the earnings and appreciation on all Roth contributions, are tax free if certain conditions are met.

ROTH IRA CHARACTERISTICS

The following is an overview of the tax characteristics of the Roth IRA.

- Contributions are not tax deductible.
  Unlike with a traditional IRA, an individual is not permitted to take an income-tax deduction for his or her Roth IRA contributions. All Roth IRA contributions are made with after-tax dollars. This means that the amount of the contribution is treated as basis in the IRA.
- Earnings are tax deferred.
  Earnings and gains from a Roth IRA are tax deferred and may be tax exempt if certain conditions are met (a "qualified distribution"). This means that no income and gains generated by a Roth IRA investment are subject to income tax.
- Tax-free earnings.
  The attraction of the Roth IRA is based on the fact that qualified distributions of Roth earnings are tax free. As long as certain conditions

are met and the distribution is a qualified distribution, the Roth IRA owner will never pay tax on any Roth distributions received.

ROTH IRA CONTRIBUTIONS—IN GENERAL

An individual may make several types of contributions, including regular, spousal, conversion, and catch-up contributions.

REGULAR CONTRIBUTIONS

In the case of a Roth IRA, there are no maximum-age restrictions for making Roth IRA contributions; however, there are income restrictions that must be met.

NO MAXIMUM- OR MINIMUM-AGE RESTRICTION

Unlike traditional IRAs, there is no maximum-age restriction for making Roth IRA contributions. As long as the individual satisfies the required-income guidelines, he or she may make Roth IRA contributions even after the age of 70½. In addition, federal law does not impose minimum-age restrictions for making Roth IRA contributions. However, typically, most financial institutions will verify the appropriate state laws relating to minors signing contracts.

WHAT IS THE ELIGIBLE COMPENSATION REQUIREMENT?

The definition of earned income for a Roth IRA is the same as a traditional IRA.

ROTH IRA CONTRIBUTIONS

A regular contribution to a Roth IRA is generally limited to the lesser of the annual contribution limit or 100 percent of the individual's compensation. The Roth IRA contribution limit is the same as the traditional IRA limit. For the year 2016, the annual Roth IRA contribution limit for an individual under the age of fifty is $5,500, and $6,500 for an individual over the age of fifty. An individual making Roth IRA contributions must reduce those contributions by the amount of any contributions made to a traditional IRA. In other words, the annual IRA contribution limit for 2016 ($5,500 or $6,500) applies to all IRAs and cannot be applied separately to one or more traditional IRAs or Roth IRAs. For example, if Jim had a traditional and a Roth IRA and was under the age of fifty, Jim could *not* make a $5,500 contribution to both his traditional IRA and Roth IRA. Jim would be limited to making a $5,500 contribution to his traditional IRA, Roth IRA, or some sort of combination contribution made to both his traditional and Roth IRA, as long as the combined contribution did not exceed $5,500 for 2016.

"When are Roth IRA contributions due?" Mike asked.

"You can make contributions for 2016 by the due date (not including extensions) for filing your 2016 tax return," John replied. "This means that most people can make contributions for 2016 up to April 15, 2017."

"The only thing I worry about, though," responded Mike, "is what if I contribute too much to my Roth IRA since these Roth calculation limits are so complicated?"

"A six percent excise tax applies to any excess contribution to a Roth IRA, said John. "But don't worry; there is a way to correct any excess contributions made."

"OK, that's a relief," Mike said.

How Do the Catch-up Contribution Rules Work for Roth IRAs?

As with a traditional IRA, an individual who turns fifty before the end of the taxable year may be eligible to make Roth IRA catch-up contributions. The maximum amount that an individual over the age of fifty may contribute annually as a catch-up contribution is $1,000 for 2016. An individual must reduce a Roth IRA contribution by any catch-up contribution made to a traditional IRA.

CAN I MAKE ROTH IRA CONTRIBUTIONS IF I HAVE NO ELIGIBLE COMPENSATION BUT MY SPOUSE DOES?

As with a traditional IRA contribution, an individual with no eligible compensation but who is married may generally make a Roth IRA contribution based on his or her spouse's compensation. This is often referred to as a "spousal contribution."

TAX ADVANTAGES OF USING A ROTH IRA

It always comes down to the taxes. With a Roth IRA, as long as you have some patience, can wait until you are over 59½, and have had the Roth IRA open at least five years, all Roth IRA contributions, income, and appreciation will be tax-free. That means no federal or state income tax, ever, upon withdrawal, and it means not simply tax-deferred growth but tax-free growth. "As a tax attorney, I have to say, things don't get much better than that," John said.

In order to get a better handle on the potential advantages of making after-tax Roth contributions, it is helpful to run several possible scenarios:

Example 1

Starting balance: $0
Annual contribution: $1,500
Current age: 35
Age of retirement: 70
Expected rate of return: 8 percent
Marginal tax rate: 25 percent
Total amount of contributions: $52,000

At age 70, with a Roth IRA, the individual would have $279,153 tax-free and a tax savings of $177,181.

Example 2

Starting balance: $0
Annual contribution: $5,500
Current age: 30
Age of retirement: 65
Expected rate of return: 9.77 percent
Marginal tax rate: 25 percent
Total amount of contributions: $192,000

At age 65, with a Roth IRA, the individual would have $1,552,705.118 tax-free and a tax savings of $876,642.

Example 3

Now, assuming the individual wanted to retire at age 70:
Starting balance: $0
Annual contribution: $5,500
Current age: 30
Age of retirement: 70
Expected rate of return: 9.77 percent
Marginal tax rate: 25 percent
Total amount of contributions: $200,000

At age 70, with a Roth IRA, the individual would have $2,510,367 tax-free and a tax savings of $1,282,637.

Example 4

Starting balance: $0
Annual contribution: $3,500
Current age: 38

Age of retirement: 70
Expected rate of return: 8 percent
Marginal tax rate: 25 percent
Total amount of contributions: $112,000

At age 70, with a Roth IRA, the individual would have $507,327 tax-free and a tax savings of $337,201.

ROTH IRA DISTRIBUTIONS

"The difference between a traditional IRA and a Roth IRA is most evident in the treatment of distributions. Don't worry; we will go through the Roth IRA distribution rules in greater detail down the road," John said.

As a brief reminder, in the case of a traditional IRA, an IRA distribution is taxed as ordinary income unless it is rolled over into another retirement plan. If the individual is under the age of 59½ when the distribution is made, a 10 percent excise tax would apply to the distribution in addition to the ordinary income tax due on the value of the distribution. If the individual is over the age of 70½ at the time the distribution is taken, then no excise tax applies; however, the individual is required to pay ordinary income tax on the amount of the traditional IRA distribution. Remember also that an individual over the age of 70½ is required to take minimum annual distributions based on a percentage of the individual's total IRA value at the end of the year. Each year, the IRS releases a table that determines the amount of the required minimum distribution.

DETERMINING THE TAX STATUS OF ROTH IRA DISTRIBUTIONS: THE ORDERING RULES

In order to determine which contributions, rollovers, or earnings are distributed from a Roth IRA, the IRS has established a set of ordering rules. Under the ordering rules, the first Roth IRA assets distributed are considered to be a return of the amounts contributed to the Roth IRA. Once the total Roth IRA contributions made have been completely distributed, the ordering rules require that the next assets to be distributed are rollover or conversion amounts (excluding designed Roth IRA account rollovers), if any. Once all those types of assets have been distributed, any further Roth IRA distributions would come from any earnings accumulated by the Roth IRA investments.

AREN'T ALL ROTH IRA DISTRIBUTIONS TAX-FREE? SHOULD I CARE ABOUT THE ORDERING RULES?

Yes and no. If an individual is over the age of 59½ and the Roth IRA account has been established for at least five years, then any distributions from a Roth IRA would be tax-free (qualified distributions). However, in the case of a nonqualified distribution (discussed below in more detail), the ordering of the distributions is significant because of the different tax and penalty consequences that could apply based on the type of asset distributed (i.e., Roth IRA contributions, which are always nontaxable, versus Roth IRA earnings, which may be taxable).

The following is a summary of the Roth IRA ordering-distribution rules and the tax and penalty that may apply.

Order of Roth IRA Assets for Distribution	"Qualified" Distribution	"Nonqualified" Distribution
Amount contributed to Roth IRA	Not subject to tax or penalty	Not subject to tax or penalty
Amounts converted to a Roth IRA that were subject to tax	Not subject to tax or penalty	Not subject to tax but subject to a 10% early distribution penalty
Amounts converted to a Roth IRA that were not subject to tax	Not subject to tax or penalty	Not subject to tax or penalty
Roth IRA earnings and investments gains	Not subject to tax or penalty	Subject to tax and 10% early distribution penalty

WHAT IS A QUALIFIED ROTH IRA DISTRIBUTION?

A qualified distribution from a Roth IRA is not subject to tax or penalty when made. To have a qualified distribution, the Roth IRA owner must have satisfied a "five-year waiting period" (starting with the first taxable year in which the Roth IRA owner made a contribution to any Roth IRA) and must meet any one of the following requirements:

- reached the age of 59½;
- qualify as disabled;
- qualify as a first-time homebuyer ($10,000 limitation); or
- death.

HOW IS THE FIVE-YEAR WAITING PERIOD CALCULATED?

In order for a Roth IRA distribution to be a qualified distribution, one of the requirements is that the Roth IRA owner must have satisfied a five-year waiting period (starting with the first taxable year in which the Roth IRA owner made a contribution to any Roth IRA). For purposes of calculating the five-year rule, all Roth IRA accounts are treated as one account. Therefore, as long as an individual has made a contribution to a Roth IRA, the five-year waiting period would begin running at that point.

For example, Joe established a Roth IRA in 2007 at age fifty-five and made a contribution of $1,000. In 2013, at age sixty-one, Joe decided to establish another Roth IRA. Because Joe established a Roth IRA account more than five years ago, Joe has already satisfied the five-year rule and would thus be able to take distributions of after-tax contributions and investment income and gains from either Roth IRA tax-free, even the recent Roth IRA that was opened less than five years ago.

HELPFUL TIP

Even if you do not currently have any interest in opening a Roth IRA, you may at some point, so if you are under 59½, you may want to establish a Roth IRA with just a minimal amount, even one dollar, just to start the five-year waiting period. This way, if you ever want to make Roth IRA contributions in the future, you would have already likely satisfied the five-year waiting period; and as long as you are over 59½, you would be able to take distributions of after-tax contributions and investment income and gains from your Roth IRA(s) tax-free. Note: There are separate five-year waiting periods in the case of Roth IRA conversions.

DISTRIBUTION OF AFTER-TAX CONTRIBUTIONS

In the case of a Roth IRA, the amount you contribute is never subject to tax when it comes out. Even if you take it a day after you contribute it and are under 59½, the amount you contributed to your Roth IRA is never subject to tax. The reason for this is simple—you already paid tax on that amount, so the IRS isn't going to tax it again. Remember, in the case of a traditional IRA, the amount you contribute is pretax—meaning you have not paid tax on that amount and, in fact, you have likely received a tax-deduction for the contribution amount, which is why the contribution amount will be subject to tax upon withdrawal.

Because Roth contributions are never subject to tax upon withdrawal, any distribution taken from a Roth IRA is considered to be a return of your Roth IRA contributions until all Roth IRA contributions you have made over the years have been withdrawn. This rule applies to all Roth IRA contributions you have made, even if you have more than one Roth IRA. This means that all Roth IRA contributions are withdrawn tax-free before Roth IRA earnings are recovered. Therefore, once you make a Roth IRA contribution, you will always be able to withdraw that money tax-free. For this reason, some people use the Roth IRA as an emergency fund. If they ever get into a financial jam and need money, they will always have the ability to withdraw the Roth IRA contributions tax-free and without penalty, which would not be the case if a traditional IRA contribution was made.

For example, Joe began making Roth IRA contributions of $5,000 each year beginning in 2006. By the beginning of 2011, Joe's Roth IRA had grown to $35,000. Of that amount, $25,000 was from Joe's annual contributions and $10,000 was from investment gains. In March 2011, Joe was in a difficult financial position and needed additional funds to help pay some personal bills. Joe decided to withdraw $25,000 from his Roth IRA. The $25,000 was not subject to tax because Joe's distribution was deemed to be a return of his contributions. However, if Joe decided to withdraw $30,000, the first $25,000 would be tax-free because it would be a return of his contributions. The excess $5,000 would be subject to income tax and a 10 percent excise tax if Joe was under the age of 59½ and the Roth IRA had been open for less than five years.

What Is a Nonqualified Distribution?

Any distribution from a Roth IRA that is not treated as a "qualified" distribution is by default treated as a "nonqualified" distribution—in other words, nonqualified distributions would occur if the five-year waiting period has not been satisfied or if one of the qualifying events has *not* occurred:

- reaching the age 59½;
- qualifying as disabled;
- qualifying as a first-time home buyer (up to a lifetime $10,000 limitation); or
- death.

How Are Nonqualified Distributions Treated?

A nonqualified distribution is treated much like a traditional IRA distribution. The Roth IRA contributions you made will always come out tax-free, but the earnings generated by your Roth IRA will be subject to income tax.

No Required Minimum Distributions

Unlike a traditional IRA, a Roth IRA owner is never required to take a Roth IRA distribution. In other words, the required minimum distribution rules do not apply to Roth IRA owners. This is one of the main differences between a traditional IRA and a Roth IRA.

DIFFERENCES BETWEEN A TRADITIONAL IRA AND A ROTH IRA

"I am sure that most of what I just described about the traditional and a Roth IRA seems a bit confusing and is starting to make your head spin. Don't worry; you are not alone. For that reason, I want you to have this chart, which summarizes the main differences between a traditional and a Roth IRA." John told Mike he was going to e-mail him a chart that summarized the main differences between a traditional IRA and a Roth IRA.

Traditional IRA	Roth IRA
Tax-deductible contributions.	Contributions are not tax deductible. Contributions made to a Roth IRA are from after-tax dollars.
Distributions may be taken by age 59½ and are mandatory by 70½.	No mandatory distribution age. With a Roth IRA, you are not required to take distributions ever.
Taxes are paid on amount of distributions (10 percent excise tax may apply if withdrawn prior to age 59½).	No taxes on distributions if rules and regulations are followed.
Available to everyone; no income restrictions with earned income.	• For 2016, subject to adjustments each year, Single filers, Heads of Household, or those Married Filing Separately (and you did not live with your spouse during the year) with modified adjusted gross income up to $132,000 can make a full contribution. Contributions are phased out starting at $117,000, and you cannot make a contribution if your adjusted gross income is in excess of $132,000.

	• Joint filers with modified adjusted gross income up to $194,000 can make a full contribution. Once again, this contribution is phased out starting at $184,000, and you cannot make a contribution if your adjusted gross income is in excess of $194,000.
Funds can be used to purchase a variety of investments (stocks, real estate, precious metals, notes, etc.).	Funds can be used to purchase a variety of investments (stocks, real estate, precious metals, notes, etc.).
IRA investments grow tax-free until distribution (tax deferral)	All earnings and principal are 100 percent tax-free if rules and regulations are followed. No tax on distributions, so maximum tax-deferral.
Income/gains from IRA investments are tax-free.	Income/gains from IRA investments are tax-free.
Purchasing real estate property and then taking possession of the property after age 59½ would be subject to tax.	Purchasing domestic or foreign real estate property and then taking possession after age 59½ would be tax-free.

WHAT IS A SEP IRA?

A Simplified Employee Pension (SEP) plan provides business owners with a simplified method to contribute toward their employees' retirement as well as their own retirement savings. A SEP is essentially an employer-sponsored profit-sharing plan. Contributions are made to an individual retirement account or annuity (IRA) set up for each plan participant (a SEP IRA). The main difference between a SEP IRA, a traditional IRA, and a Roth IRA is that a SEP IRA must be established by a business, whereas traditional IRAs and Roth IRAs are established by individuals. In other words, an individual who is not an owner of a business cannot establish a SEP IRA.

A SEP IRA account is a traditional IRA and follows the same investment, distribution, and rollover rules as traditional IRAs.

Employees must be included in the SEP plan if they have:

- reached age twenty-one;
- received at least $550 in compensation from your business for the year; and
- worked for your business in at least three of the last five years.

The three-of-five eligibility rule means you must include any employee in your plan who has worked for you in any three of the last five years (as long as the employee has satisfied the other plan-eligibility requirements). This is the most restrictive eligibility requirement allowable. You can choose to use less-restrictive participation rules in your plan, such as allowing employees to participate immediately after they start work or after a shorter period of employment. If you use the three-of-five rule, you must count any work, no matter how little, in each of the previous five years. Use plan years (often the calendar year), not years based on the date the employee started working for you.

John said, "Using the three-of-five rule is a nifty way for business owners to make SEP IRA contributions for themselves without having to make contributions for their employees. However, once the three-of-five rule is met, the employer is required to provide all eligible employees with equal-percentage profit-sharing contributions."

"So, the three-of-five rule could help the business owner out for a couple of years, but after that, the employer is required to provide all eligible employees with a SEP IRA contribution using the same percentage it used for the business owner?" asked Mike.

"That is correct," John said.

"How do the contributions work?" Mike asked.

"The contributions you make to each employee's SEP IRA each year cannot exceed the lesser of:

- 25 percent of compensation (20 percent in the case of a sole proprietorship of single-member LLC); or
- $53,000 for 2016.

"There are *no* catch-up contributions for a SEP IRA as there are for a 401(k) plan," John added.

These limits apply to contributions you make for your employees to all defined contribution plans, which includes SEPs. Compensation up to $265,000 in 2016 of an employee's compensation may be considered for contribution purposes. Also, contributions must be made in cash, and you cannot contribute property.

WHAT IS A SIMPLE IRA?

A SIMPLE (savings incentive match plan for employees) IRA plan allows employees and employers to contribute to traditional IRAs set up for employees. Like a SEP IRA, a SIMPLE IRA can only be established by a business. Employees may choose to make salary-reduction contributions, and the employer is required to make either matching or nonelective contributions. Contributions are made to an individual retirement account or annuity (IRA) set up for each employee (a SIMPLE IRA).

A SIMPLE IRA plan account is an IRA and follows the same investment, distribution, and rollover rules as a traditional IRA.

Any employer (including self-employed individuals, tax-exempt organizations, and governmental entities) that had no more than one hundred employees with $5,000 or more in compensation during the preceding calendar year (the "hundred-employee limitation") can establish a SIMPLE IRA plan. You can set up a SIMPLE IRA plan effective any date between January 1 and October 1, provided you (or any predecessor employer) didn't previously maintain a SIMPLE IRA plan. If you're a new employer that came into existence after October 1 of the year, you can establish the SIMPLE IRA plan as soon as administratively feasible after your business came into existence.

All employees who received at least $5,000 in compensation from you during any two preceding calendar years (whether or not consecutive) and who are reasonably expected to receive at least $5,000 in compensation during the calendar year are eligible to participate in the SIMPLE IRA plan for the current calendar year.

Each eligible employee may make a salary-reduction contribution, and the employer must make either a matching contribution or a nonelective contribution.

An employee may defer up to $12,500 in 2016 (subject to cost-of-living adjustments for later years).

Employees age fifty or over can make a catch-up contribution of up to $3,000 in 2016 (subject to cost-of-living adjustments for later years).

With respect to employer contributions, the employer is generally required to either

- match each employee's salary-reduction contribution on a dollar-for-dollar basis up to 3 percent of the employee's compensation (not limited by the annual compensation limit); or
- make nonelective contributions of 2 percent of the employee's compensation up to the annual limit of $265,000 for 2016, subject to cost-of-living adjustments in later years).

If you choose to make nonelective contributions, you must make them for all eligible employees whether or not they make salary-reduction contributions.

With respect to the 3 percent match, you may elect to reduce the 3 percent matching contributions for a calendar year, but only if

- the limit isn't reduced below 1 percent;
- the limit isn't reduced for more than two years out of the five-year period that ends with (and includes) the year for which the election is effective; and
- you notify employees of the reduced limit within a reasonable time before the sixty-day election period during which employees can enter into salary-reduction agreements.

Generally, the same tax results apply to distributions from a SIMPLE IRA as to distributions from a regular IRA with one notable exception. During the two-year period, you may transfer an amount in a SIMPLE IRA to another SIMPLE IRA in a tax-free trustee-to-trustee transfer. If, during this two-year period, an amount is paid from a SIMPLE IRA directly to another IRA that is not a SIMPLE IRA, then the payment is treated as a distribution from the SIMPLE IRA and a contribution to the other IRA that doesn't qualify as a rollover contribution. After the expiration of the two-year period, you may transfer an amount in a SIMPLE IRA to any IRA or 401(k) plan without tax. In addition, a SIMPLE IRA has an exclusive-plan rule, which does not allow a business to adopt both a SIMPLE IRA and a Solo 401(k) plan in the same taxable year, whereas a business can adopt both a SEP IRA and a 401(k) plan.

"I hope this call wasn't too painful for you," John joked.

"Not too bad," Mike responded.

"As a recap," John surmised, "the foundation of retirement investing is based on the concept of tax deferral. Tax deferral means that you can postpone taxes on any earnings you make on the money in your tax-deferred accounts. That means your money is growing each year without having to remove any funds to pay tax. For example, if you contributed $2,000 to a traditional IRA each year for ten years and averaged a 7 percent annual rate of return, assuming a 25 percent income-tax rate, your traditional IRA would be worth $31,291, whereas if you invested the funds personally, you would have just $23,468. Now, imagine that instead of contributing over ten years, you contributed over thirty years. Assuming the same facts, your traditional IRA would be worth $244,692 versus just $183,519. Pretty impressive numbers for just saving around $5 a day. If a traditional IRA was used, you would eventually have to pay the taxes on the income deferred. But here's the good news. You may be in a lower tax bracket in retirement, so the taxes you pay will be less than if you had paid them during your working years, and you only pay tax on the amount you withdraw from your tax-deferred accounts. The rest of the money in your tax-deferred account continues to grow tax deferred—and compound interest continues to work its magic over time. Of course, you could always open a Roth IRA, assuming you satisfied the income limitations, and all your income and gains would be tax-free, assuming you were over the age of 59½ when you took a Roth IRA distribution and the Roth IRA had been open at least five years. The thing with tax deferral is that, generally, the earlier you start, the greater the tax deferral power will be."

"One last thing I wanted to ask you—is it better to make pretax or Roth IRA contributions," Mike said.

SHOULD I MAKE ROTH OR PRETAX CONTRIBUTIONS?

Often tax professionals and financial advisers are asked whether it makes sense to make a Roth after-tax contribution or a pretax contribution. The upside with Roth contributions is that your Roth withdrawals in retirement (including any earnings and gains on your Roth contributions) are completely federal income-tax free if you meet certain requirements.

When deciding whether you should make Roth contributions, pretax contributions, or a combination of the two, here are some important considerations.

If you feel your tax rate in retirement will be higher than it is today, Roth contributions may make sense for you. If you expect your tax rate to be lower in retirement than during your working years, you may benefit more from making before-tax contributions and paying taxes when you withdraw your money. It is hard to imagine now, but we are currently in a historically low tax-rate environment. For most of the century, including some boom times, top-bracket income-tax rates were much higher than they are today. In fact, during the 1950s and early 1960s, the top-bracket income-tax rate was over 90 percent. In light of our growing deficit, Social Security shortfall, and heavy government spending, it is not far off to suggest that income-tax rates will be higher when you retire than they are now. Of course, no one knows what will happen tomorrow when it comes to Congress and taxes, and especially not in twenty or thirty years, so an educated guess is all one can make.

How confident are you in your expected returns? If you are very confident that your investments and/or cash flow from your investments are relatively secure and will grow over time, a Roth account would make sense. Bear in mind that many people felt that Enron, Lehman Brothers, and Bear Stearns were safe investments and suitable for Roth funds, and we all know how those companies turned out. In general, Roth IRA investments seem to work well with real-estate-income-producing investments as well as dividend-growth investments in which the cash flows are generally perceived as stable.

The further away your retirement, the greater the opportunity for tax-free growth and the more potential you have for tax-free gains. Basically, if you will not be retiring in the near future, Roth contributions may make a good deal of sense, since your account potentially has more time to grow in value. This may make the tax advantages of Roth contributions even more important to you—although Roth dollars can benefit retirement savers of all ages.

IMPORTANT CONSIDERATIONS IN DETERMINING WHETHER TO MAKE PRETAX IRA OR AFTER-TAX (ROTH) IRA CONTRIBUTIONS

Pre-tax Contribution	After-Tax (Roth) contribution
Tax deductible contributions	Contributions are not tax deductible – contributions made to a Roth IRA are from after tax dollars
Distributions may be taken by age 59½. and are mandatory by 70 1/2.	No Mandatory Distribution Age – with a Roth IRA you are not required to ever take distributions
Taxes are paid on amount of distributions (10% excise tax may apply if withdrawn prior to age 59½.)	No taxes on distributions if rules and regulations are followed
Available to everyone; no income restrictions with earned income	• For 2015, subject to adjustments each year, Single filers, Head of Household or Married Filing Separately (and you did not live with your spouse during the year) with modified adjusted gross income up to $131,000 can make a full contribution. Contributions are phased-out starting at $116,000 and you cannot make a contribution if your adjusted gross income is in excess of $131,000. • Joint filers with modified adjusted gross income up to $193,000 can make a full contribution. Once again, this contribution is phased-out starting at $183,000 and you cannot make a contribution if your adjusted gross income is in excess of $193,000.
Funds can be used to purchase a variety of investments (stocks, real estate, precious metals, notes, etc.)	Funds can be used to purchase a variety of investments (stocks, real estate, precious metals, notes, etc.)
IRA investments grow tax-free until distribution (tax deferral)	All earnings and principal are 100% tax free if rules and regulations are followed – No tax on distributions so maximum tax-deferral
Income/gains from IRA investments are tax-free	Income/gains from IRA investments are tax-free
Purchasing a real estate property than taking possession of the property after 59½. would be subject to tax	Purchasing a domestic or foreign real estate property then taking possession after 59/1/2 would be tax-free

"Thanks so much, John, for giving me all this great info," Mike said.

"My pleasure—call me next week same time and we can chat about some of the main advantages of the self-directed IRA and how to make investments with it," John said.

3

THE SELF-DIRECTED IRA—BENEFITS & INVESTMENTS

Mike called John the next week. John was eager to get started and dove right into discussing the idea of the self-directed IRA.

WHAT IS A SELF-DIRECTED IRA

"There are around forty-nine million IRAs in existence today. Believe it or not, most of those forty-nine million IRAs could be considered self-directed IRAs."

"Wait," Mike said. "Are you saying that most IRA holders are using their IRAs to invest in real estate, precious metals, tax liens, or private businesses?"

"No," John answered. "Even if it's allowed under IRS rules, they're not doing that. But what I am saying is that the majority of all IRA investments are technically self-directed since the IRA holder is typically the one who determines what type of investments will be made with his or her IRA."

"You mean, the way I select the mutual funds or even stocks that my IRA purchases?"

"Exactly. When you decide which investments to make using your IRA, you are technically self-directing your IRA investment. I wish that more people knew, however, that the IRS allows them to do more than simply select mutual funds or stocks to buy when making IRA investments."

"But I'm getting the feeling that not all IRAs, even those that are technically self-directed, would allow me to make real estate investments."

"That's correct. Whether an IRA is a self-directed IRA depends on two factors—control and investment opportunities."

"My wife's IRA is through a local bank, and I am invested in mutual funds, so I doubt they will allow me to buy real estate or make other alternative-asset investments," Mike said.

1. FINANCIAL INSTITUTION SELF-DIRECTED IRA

"Correct again," John responded. "The 'traditional financial institution' self-directed IRA is by far the most popular type of self-directed IRA. Like your Roth IRA, the majority of all IRAs are held at traditional financial institutions, such as Fidelity, Vanguard, Charles Schwab, Bank of America, Merrill Lynch, and so on. Many traditional financial institutions advertise themselves as offering a self-directed IRA, but what that really means is that you will be limited to purchasing stocks, mutual funds, bonds, and other traditional types of investments that earn the institution commissions. In other words, you need the consent of your IRA custodian before making an investment."

"As a reminder," he continued, "a custodian is your IRA trustee. Basically, that's the institution that holds your IRA account, in your case your local bank. By law, every retirement account must be held at a custodian or trustee. A trustee may be a bank, trust company, credit union, or a large brokerage firm that is licensed by the IRS. IRS regulations require that either a qualified trustee or custodian hold the IRA assets on behalf of the IRA owner."

"Are there some IRA custodians that will allow you to invest your retirement funds in real estate and other alternative assets?" Mike asked

"Yes. A true self-directed IRA custodian is known as a passive custodian— and a passive custodian allows the IRA holder to engage in nontraditional investments like real estate, but these IRA custodians do not sell financial investments or offer investment advice, like a Schwab or Chase."

"So, to get this straight," Mike said, "when you have a self-directed IRA at a traditional financial institution, you're technically able to self-direct your IRA investments. But you're probably limited to investing in the financial products offered by the financial institution."

"That's right," John answered. "For example, a financial institution such as Vanguard or Fidelity will allow you to select the type of investments for your own IRA, but your choices are generally limited to the financial products they offer—in other words—stocks, mutual funds, and bonds. They won't permit you to make alternative-asset investments such as real estate, precious metals, private business investments, foreign currency, and options."

"Why won't they allow me to purchase real estate with my IRA if it's permitted by the IRS," asked Mike."

"It's just business," he answered. "Financial institutions are in business to earn profit and generate strong earnings for shareholders. Like any business, they're motivated to enhance the bottom line."

"In other words," Mike summed up, "they don't make any money by allowing you to purchase real estate or other alternative-asset investments, so it doesn't make any sense to let you do that."

"Exactly," was the answer. "If they could make money when you bought real estate with your IRA funds, they'd probably allow you to do that. But when an IRA holder buys real estate, the parties that benefit from the investment are the seller of the property, the real estate agent, the title-insurance company, and the closing attorney. On the other hand, if an IRA holder uses IRA assets to purchase mutual funds or stocks, the financial institution selling you those stocks benefits directly from the investment."

"So," said Mike, "if they let you shift your IRA assets away from financial products that generate their fees and commissions, such as mutual funds, to nontraditional investments such as real estate, that's going to negatively affect the financial institution's bottom line."

"Right," deduced John. "It'll reduce the financial institution's profits for sure and probably put a strain on its financial reserves. So, most traditional financial institutions just don't allow it."

BENEFITS OF USING A SELF-DIRECTED IRA

"Before you get into how you can make self-directed IRA investments, what are some of the benefits of using a self-directed IRA?" Mike asked.

"Good question. Here's my answer."

A. DIVERSIFICATION

With the self-directed IRA or Roth IRA, you can invest in almost any type of investment, including real estate, allowing you to diversify and better protect your retirement portfolio. If the 2008 financial crisis had any positive features, it was that many Americans started asking about alternative investment options for their retirement accounts. Diversification is a strategy to help make sure all your retirement assets aren't concentrated in a certain type of investment or area.

Retirement-account diversification has become a popular concept for many retirement-account holders. It is believed that the financial crisis cost retirees almost 25 percent of their retirement assets, and many are still trying to get back to where they were before the crisis. The sudden and steep stock-market fall, coupled with the lack of faith in Wall Street and the global financial markets, caused many Americans to seek a more balanced and diversified retirement portfolio. This shift brought a sharp increase in the number of Americans looking at self-directed IRAs as vehicles for attaining a level of account diversification. Accordingly, balance and diversification have become popular hallmarks of a strong investment-retirement portfolio.

Alternative investments such as real estate have always been permitted in IRAs; it even says so right on the IRS website. But few people seemed to know about this option until the last several years. The alternative-asset and self-directed retirement markets were relatively small and unknown prior to 2008. A few small groups of early adopters in the retirement world had heard about the nontraditional-asset option and took advantage of it to buy real estate and other nontraditional assets. These groups were on the cutting edge of investment options and largely did not have an impact on the greater retirement-investment community. The crossover only started after the 2008 financial crisis, when many Americans actively set out to determine whether alternative-investment options were available to them rather than waiting for these options to be advertised or offered.

After the 2008 financial crisis, allocating a portion of an investment portfolio to alternative-asset investments, such as real estate or precious metals, was seen as a way to help diversify a retirement-investment portfolio of stocks and bonds and reduce risk. Alternative-asset investments for retirement accounts were also shown to provide an income stream and hedge against inflation.

Of course, there is no certainty that a diversified investment-retirement portfolio will provide greater benefits to stockholders than a portfolio that is more concentrated in any particular individual real estate investment sector or location. History still suggests that stocks are a solid investment over the long term. For example, according to historical records, the average annual return for the S&P 500 since its inception in 1928, through 2014, is approximately 10 percent. However, that number can be very misleading. Accurate calculations of average returns, taking all significant factors into account, can be challenging. Nevertheless, having your retirement account properly diversified and not wholly subjected to the ups and downs of Wall Street has become a priority since the 2008 financial crisis and is one of the factors behind the emergence of the self-directed IRA solution.

B. INVEST IN SOMETHING YOU UNDERSTAND

Many Americans became frustrated with the equity markets after the 2008 financial crisis. Thankfully, we have seen the financial markets rebound since then and have even seen some years of over 20 percent growth in the equity markets. Nevertheless, many Americans are still somewhat shell-shocked from the market swings and not 100 percent sure what exactly happens on Wall Street and how it all works. Real estate, in comparison, is often a more comfortable investment for the lower and middle classes because they grew up exposed to it, whereas the upper classes often learned about Wall Street and other securities during their younger years and college days. Everyone has heard someone talk about the importance of owning a home or the amount of money that can be made by owning real estate—from Donald Trump to reality-TV stars. Real estate is fast becoming mainstream and one of the most trusted asset classes for Americans. It is, of course, not without risk, but many retirement investors feel more comfortable understanding the real estate market, and buying and selling real estate, than they do stocks.

C. INFLATION PROTECTION

Rising food and energy prices, coupled with high federal debt levels and low interest rates, have recently fueled new inflationary fears. As a result, some investors may be looking for ways to protect their portfolios from the ravages of inflation. It is a matter of guesswork to estimate whether these inflation risks are real, but for some retirement investors, protecting retirement assets from inflation is a big concern. Inflation can have a nasty impact on a retirement portfolio because it means a dollar today may not be worth a dollar tomorrow. Inflation also increases the cost of things that are necessary for humans to live and enjoy life, such as food, gas, shelter, clothing, and medical services, decreasing the value of money so that goods and services cost more. For example, if someone has an IRA worth $250,000 at a time of high inflation, that $250,000 will be worth significantly less or have significantly less buying power. This can mean the difference between retiring and working the rest of your life. Buying hard assets is seen as one way of protecting your assets against inflation. Many investors have long recognized that investing in commercial real estate or precious metals can provide a natural protection against inflation, as rents tend to increase when prices do, acting as a hedge against inflation.

D. HARD ASSETS

Many nontraditional assets, such as real estate and precious metals, are tangible hard assets that you can see and touch. With real estate, for example, you can drive by with your family, point out the window, and say, "I own that." For some, that's important psychologically, especially in times of financial instability, inflation, or political or global upheaval.

E. TAX-FREE WEALTH FOR YOUR RETIREMENT

The Roth IRA is truly the best legal tax shelter available, and it is accessible to everyone. Remember, a Roth IRA is an after-tax account wherein no tax deduction is received on the contribution, but all income and gains associated with the Roth IRA are tax-free in general, as long as the Roth IRA has been open at least five years and the Roth IRA holder is at least age 59½. Along with the great tax benefits of generating tax-free asset growth and income, especially in light of an expected higher-tax environment in the near future, the Roth IRA can serve as a valuable estate-planning tool by allowing you to pass tax-free wealth on to your heirs.

Using retirement funds to make alternative-asset investments is not for everyone. That said, buying real estate or other alternative assets with retirement funds through a self-directed IRA or Roth IRA is an option that more and more people are starting to consider. According to the data provider Preqin,[2] the alternative-assets industry's leading source of data and intelligence, the alternative-assets industry added more than $600 billion in assets under management in 2015 and, as of January 2015, the assets under management of alternative-asset classes now stand at $6.9 trillion.

Certainly, the 2008 financial crisis had a large impact on many Americans looking to alternative assets as a source of diversification. These numbers are even more impressive when you consider that the alternative-asset investment market is not advertised to the average American, especially when it comes to retirement accounts. When is the last time you saw a TV commercial from a major bank or financial institution proclaiming an opportunity to buy real estate or gold through your IRA? Those institutions do not allow their IRA accounts to invest in any alternative-asset class for the simple reason that they don't make money when you purchase real estate or other alternative assets, but they do make money when you buy their financial products. The genie is now out of the bottle, and more and more American retirement investors are starting to learn about the self-directed IRA and Roth IRA and some of the exciting retirement, tax, and investment benefits they present.

"So tell me about the financial institutions that allow me to make nontraditional investments with my IRA funds, such as real estate," Mike requested.

---

2. https://www.preqin.com/docs/reports/Preqin-Investor-Outlook-Alternative-Assets-H1-2015.pdf.

"OK," John said. "There are two kinds of those, too. I have already gone into some detail on these, but I think it is worthwhile to spend a little more time on the difference between using a custodian-controlled self-directed IRA versus a checkbook control IRA LLC," John said.

2. CUSTODIAN-CONTROLLED SELF-DIRECTED IRAS WITHOUT CHECKBOOK CONTROL

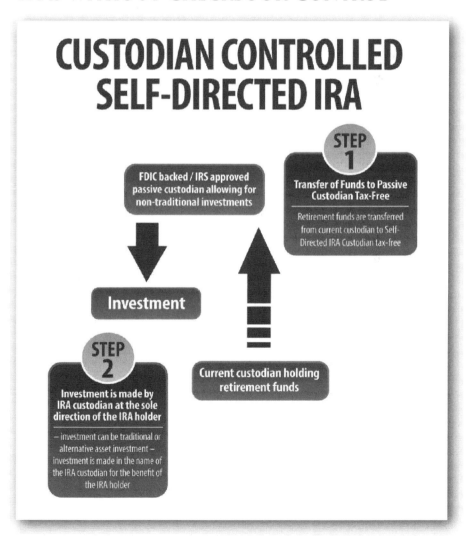

"Unlike the traditional financial institutions such as Fidelity, Vanguard, Charles Schwab, or Bank of America, there are a number of financial institutions or IRA custodians that do allow IRA holders to make nontraditional investments with their IRA funds, such as IRA Financial Trust Company and Equity Trust. They have a slightly different business model than the traditional financial institution, such as Vanguard or Wells Fargo. Unlike a traditional financial institution, which makes the majority of its IRA-related earnings from commissions and fees associated with stocks, mutual funds, bonds, and other equity- or debt-type investments, these custodians typically generate their profits through annual account valuation fees and transaction fees."

"OK," Mike answered, "so they charge you an annual fee or a fee whenever you do something with your money, or both?"

"Exactly," responded Mike. "They generally permit you to make alternative-asset investments such as real estate. So, before engaging in an IRA investment, they require you to get the consent of the custodian. You'll need to provide the custodian with the transaction documents for review as part of their transaction-review process. And even upon approval, your IRA investment would be made in the name of the custodian for the benefit of ("FBO") the IRA holder's IRA. So, for example, ABC Trust Company FBO Amy Jones IRA. In general, unlike a typical financial institution, most IRA custodians generate fees simply by opening and maintaining IRA accounts and do not offer any financial investment products or platforms. With a custodian-controlled self-directed IRA, the IRA funds are generally held with the IRA custodian and the IRA custodian, at the IRA holder's direction, will then invest those IRA funds accordingly. In addition, the fees for a custodian-controlled self-directed IRA tend to be based on the IRA account value and tend to range between $360 and $1,500. There are, of course, additional fees for transactions. The reason for this is that, with a custodian-controlled self-directed IRA, the IRA custodian is involved directly in executing the IRA investment, including signing all related transaction documentation, which is time consuming. That said, the custodian-controlled self-directed IRA is generally a really nice option for investors making one-off investments, such a land purchase, a private business investment, or a fund-type investment." John said.

3. THE SELF-DIRECTED IRA LLC WITH CHECKBOOK CONTROL

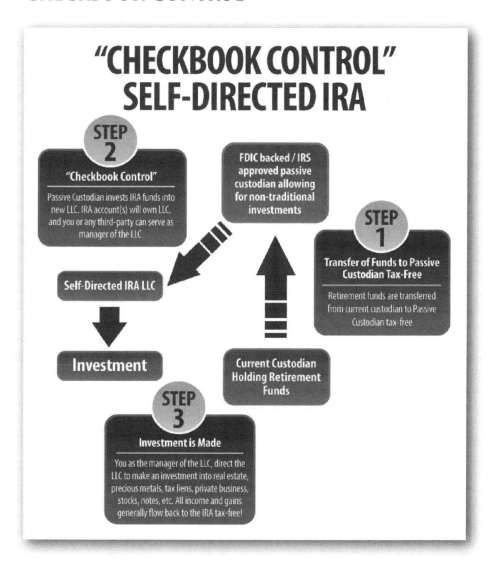

"Beginning in the mid-1990s," John laid out, "a new type of self-directed IRA structure started taking shape, allowing the IRA holder to make IRA investments directly without seeking the consent of a custodian. Unlike a custodian-controlled self-directed IRA, which requires the IRA holder to seek the consent of the custodian before making investments, with a self-directed IRA LLC with checkbook control, a limited liability company (LLC) is established that is owned by the IRA account and managed by the IRA account holder. A passive custodian then transfers the IRA holder's IRA funds to the LLC's bank account providing the IRA holder, as manager of the LLC, with checkbook control over his or her IRA funds."

"In the 1996 case of *Swanson vs. Commissioner*, 106 T.C. 76 (1996)," he continued, "the Tax Court gave its blessing to a new type of self-directed IRA structure—the self-directed IRA LLC also known as the checkbook IRA. The *Swanson* case confirmed that the ability to invest retirement funds in a newly established special purpose entity owned 100 percent by an IRA and managed by the IRA holder is legal and not a prohibited transaction. In 2001, IRS Field Service Advice (FSA) Memorandum 200128011 was released, and it was the first IRS-drafted opinion that confirmed the ruling of *Swanson*, which held that the funding of a new entity by an IRA for self-directing assets was not a prohibited transaction pursuant to IRC Section 4975. However, only recently did the Tax Court confirm that the use of a newly established limited liability company ("LLC"), wholly owned by an IRA and managed by the IRA holder, would not trigger a prohibited transaction. In October 2013, the Tax Court in T.L. Ellis, TC Memo. 2013-245, Dec. 59,674(M) ("TC Memo 2013-245") held that establishing a special-purpose limited liability company to make an investment did not trigger a prohibited transaction, as a newly established LLC cannot be deemed a disqualified person pursuant to IRC Section 4975."

"So," John surmised, "with a 'truly' self-directed IRA, the IRA holder has total control over his or her IRA funds."

"No need to get custodian consent?" Mike asked.

"Right. You no longer have to get each investment approved by the custodian of the account. Instead, all your investment decisions are made by you, as the manager of the LLC, or by any third-party manager you assign. All LLC investments are made by you as a manager, and it is as simple as writing a check. It is really as simple as that. Once a self-directed IRA account is established, you would have your retirement funds transferred or rolled into the new self-directed IRA account. At that point, once the LLC has been established, you would simply open a regular checking account for the LLC at any bank of your choice. You would need the LLC Articles of Organization, a tax identification number, as well as the LLC Operating Agreement. Typically, an attorney or specialized self-directed IRA facilitation firm, such as IRA Financial Group, can assist you with this. You would then need to provide the LLC bank account information to the IRA custodian who would then transfer the IRA funds to the LLC bank account. As a result, the LLC would be wholly owned by one or more IRA accounts so that all the income and gains would flow back to the IRA without tax," John said.

"Can you briefly explain how using the LLC can allow for the tax-free treatment —don't LLCs pay tax? Mike asked.

"Another great question," replied John. "Sorry, I should not have assumed that you had a knowledge of the tax treatment of LLCs. The LLC was invented in 1977, when Wyoming became the first state to enact an LLC statute. Today, all fifty states and the District of Columbia have enacted statutes that provide for the creation and governance of LLCs. Generally, the statutes contain similar basic procedures and elements that are required to establish the LLC. As a result, most businesses can be organized as LLCs in any of those jurisdictions, but laws governing LLCs can vary by location.

"In other words," John continued, "an LLC is formed under, exists, and is governed by a state statute that determines how an LLC in that state is formed, registered, and terminated. The statutes also generally provide that either the LLC adopt an Article of Organization, an Operating Agreement, or use the default provisions of the statute to determine other matters that impact the operation of the LLC."

"Are they as common as they seem?" Mike asked.

"They're very common," John answered. "According to some reports, there are close to four million LLCs in the United States. And probably a significant majority of all new entities formed in the United States are LLCs. They've really taken over from the C Corporation and S Corporation to become the most widely established entity in the United States, and everything I've read suggests the trend will accelerate as more and more people get comfortable with the LLC."

"So what are the advantages?" Mike asked.

"Initially, there was a question as to whether LLCs would be classified as partnerships, and receive favorable pass-through tax treatment, or be classified and taxed as corporations for federal income-tax purposes."

"How did it turn out?" Mike asked.

"The best of both worlds," John answered. "Generally, an LLC with two or more members that does not make an election will be treated as a partnership and receive pass-through tax treatment, and an LLC with only one member will be disregarded as a separate entity from its owner, meaning it is treated as a sole proprietorship and not taxed as a corporation."

"Sounds flexible."

"Yes, very," John agreed. "And an LLC has broad possibilities for its structure, operation, management. But each state has certain mandatory and default provisions. In general, LLC statutes are interpreted liberally in order to give maximum effect to the freedom of contract and to the enforceability of operating agreements."

"So does that limited liability aspect impact retirement funds?" Mike asked.

"That's the whole point," John said. "An LLC offers its members (who are usually its owners) limited liability for its IRAs. In other words, owners and members of the LLC are not liable for the debts, obligations, and liabilities of the LLC. Since, in most cases, your retirement account may be your most valuable asset, protecting that from attack by creditors is extremely important. By using an LLC, you can shield your IRA assets held outside the LLC from creditor attack."

"I get it," Mike said. "If I'm using my IRA funds to invest in real estate or make hard loans, I really want to shield those funds from attacks by creditors if anything goes wrong."

"Exactly," John said. "You want to invest, but you also want to protect. So structuring your self-directed IRA as an LLC can be really effective. That's why people use LLCs for a broad range of business and investment purposes."

John asked Mike to check his e-mail inbox as he just sent him an e-mail summarizing the main LLC benefits. Mike opened the email.

"Here's a good overview," John said, "that explains why an LLC is so popular for business and investment purposes and a few case studies for how it works in practice."

Mike took a look.

THE POPULARITY OF THE LLC

Why is the LLC so popular?

Because it:

- Is easy and inexpensive to form
- Is recognized by all states
- Provides limited liability for all members
- Has one level of tax for federal income tax and state income tax purposes (in most cases)
- Provides pass-through of business losses to the member or members
- Can utilize a corporate management structure
- Can have one member or multiple members
- Offers flexibility in distributing cash to the members
- Offers flexibility in allocating profits/losses to the members
- Offers flexibility in conducting business affairs
- Can exist indefinitely

"Of this list of great features, the most popular are the (1) limited liability protection and (2) the pass-through tax treatment. Let me explain further," John said.

1. LIMITED LIABILITY PROTECTION

In general, limited liability occurs when a person's financial liability or exposure is limited to a fixed sum, most commonly the value of a person's investment in a company or partnership. If a company with limited liability is sued, then the plaintiffs are suing the company, not its owners or investors. A shareholder or owner in an entity with limited liability protection, such as an LLC, is not personally liable for any of the debts of the company, other than for the value of his or her investment in that company.

The following is an example that highlights the advantages of limited liability protection in the case of a self-directed IRA.

Alan has $500,000 in a retirement account and wants to purchase real estate. Alan establishes a new LLC that will be owned 100 percent by his IRA—a self-directed IRA LLC. Alan directs his IRA passive custodian to invest $200,000 in to the new LLC and the LLC purchases the property. Each year, the property generates $20,000 of rental income tax-free. After year five, Alan has accumulated $80,000 of income in his self-directed IRA LLC account. In year six, an accident occurs on the property owned by the LLC and the LLC is sued. Unfortunately, Alan's insurance policy will not cover the entire claim. Because Alan has used an LLC to make the investment and not made the investment directly through a custodian-controlled self-directed IRA, the $300,000 of IRA assets held outside of the LLC will be shielded from creditor attack due to the limited liability feature of the LLC. If Alan had made the real estate investment directly using a custodian-controlled self-directed IRA, and not using an LLC, his entire IRA ($500,000) could have been subject to attack by creditors.

2. PASS-THROUGH TAX TREATMENT

LLCs are not taxed on any income they earn or generate. Instead, all taxable revenues and expenses are passed through to the owners of the entity, who would then be responsible for the payment of tax on those revenues or expenses. In other words, there is no federal income tax imposed on any income or gains generated by the LLC; only the owners would be subject to tax. Some states do impose a franchise tax or annual fee on the LLC, which we will examine later in this chapter.

LLC Owned by One Owner

If there is only one member in the company, the LLC is treated as a "disregarded entity" for tax purposes, and an individual owner would report the LLC's income or loss on Schedule C of his or her individual tax return. Thus, income from the LLC is taxed at the individual tax rates. In the case of a self-directed IRA LLC, we will see that there will be no individual-level tax because an IRA is exempt from tax under IRC Sections 408 and 408A for a Roth IRA.

LLC Owned by Two or More Owners

"In the case of an LLC owned by two or more owners," said John, "the LLC is treated as a partnership for federal income tax purposes. A partnership does not pay tax; its owners do (or do not, in the case of an IRA). But a partnership is still required to file a partnership tax return—IRS Form 1065. Under partnership tax treatment, each member of the LLC, as is the case for all partners of a partnership, annually receives a Form K-1 reporting the member's distributive share of the LLC's income or loss that is then reported on the member's individual income tax return."

"That was really helpful," Mike said. "I can now see why the checkbook control IRA is becoming quite popular. I assume there is no issue with its legality?" he asked.

"As confirmed in *Swanson* and later by the IRS in Field Service Advice Memorandum 200128011 and TC Memo 2013-245, using retirement funds to invest in a newly established LLC wholly owned by an IRA and managed by the IRA holder is not a prohibited transaction. In light of *Swanson* and TC memo 2013-245, it is evident that the Tax Court believes firmly that using IRA funds to invest in a newly established LLC will not trigger a prohibited transaction," John said.

"OK—thanks. What are the main advantages of the checkbook control self-directed IRA LLC?" Mike asked.

ADVANTAGES OF THE SELF-DIRECTED IRA LLC

That is a good question. Here are a few of the main advantages of the checkbook control IRA LLC:

A. **'Checkbook Control'**: With a self-directed IRA LLC, as manager of the self-directed IRA LLC you will have the ability to make IRA investments without seeking the consent of a custodian. Instead, all decisions are truly yours.

B. **Access**: With a self-directed IRA LLC, you will have direct access to your IRA funds, allowing you to make an investment quickly and efficiently. There is no need to obtain approvals from your custodian, deal with time delays in awaiting approval from your custodian, or pay any review fees. Your IRA funds will be held at a local bank instead of with a custodian you have never worked with before.

C. **Speed**: With a self-directed IRA LLC, when you find an investment that you want to make with your IRA funds, simply write a check or wire the funds straight from your self-directed IRA LLC bank account to make the investment. The self-directed IRA LLC allows you to eliminate the delays associated with a custodian-controlled self-directed IRA account, enabling you to act quickly when the right investment opportunity presents itself.

D. **Limited liability protection**: By using a self-directed IRA LLC with checkbook control, your IRA will benefit from the limited liability protection afforded by using an LLC. By using an LLC, all your IRA assets held outside the LLC will be shielded from attack. This is especially important in the case of IRA real estate investments, wherein many state statutes impose an extended statute of limitation for claims arising from defects in the design or construction of improvements to real estate."

"OK, so what are the fees like for a checkbook control self-directed IRA LLC?" Mike asked.

"That is also a good question. I have seen fees that range from $1,000 to $1,500, depending on the state where the LLC is formed. The checkbook control has a higher up-front cost, but if you keep the structure up and running for a number of years, in the long run it actually saves you money because the annual custodian fees are quite low, ranging from $180 to $300, which is much less than a custodian-controlled self-directed IRA," John said.

"Is it popular?"

"The popularity of self-directed IRA LLCs with checkbook control is increasing each year," John explained. "More and more custodians are getting more comfortable with their clients using these types of investment structures for their IRA funds.

"What do you think?" John asked.

"I think it sounds great," Mike responded.

"I have actually had a few clients use a checkbook control self-directed IRA because of the freedom and flexibility it offers," John said.

"One quick question," replied Mike. "Is there a difference between a self-directed IRA and a self-directed Roth IRA in terms of the setup of the structure?"

"No," answered John. "The only difference is that a self-directed IRA involves a pretax IRA and a self-directed Roth IRA involves a Roth IRA. Whether you elect to use a custodian-controlled self-directed IRA or a checkbook control self-directed IRA, the structures are the same; the only difference is the type of IRA that is being used."

"OK, thanks," Mike said.

MAKING INVESTMENTS WITH A SELF-DIRECTED ROTH IRA

"I assume you make self-directed Roth IRA investments the same way you would make investments with a traditional pretax self-directed IRA," Mike said.

"Absolutely," John said. "The only difference lies in the type of IRA being used and the taxation of the income and appreciation. In the case of a pretax IRA, just like a Roth IRA, all income and gains would flow back to the IRA without tax. The difference lies in the distribution rules. In general, with a pretax IRA, distributions prior to the age of 59½ are subject to income tax and a 10 percent early-distribution penalty, and distributions after the age of 59½ are just subject to income tax. In contrast, with a Roth IRA, as long as the Roth IRA has been open at least five years and the individual is over the age of 59½, there is generally no tax on any distributions from the Roth IRA.

"Sounds good."

"Before we get into all the investments you can make with a self-directed IRA, I think it would make sense to spend some time on the investments you are not allowed to make with your IRA. I think we covered a lot of material on our call today, so can we chat tomorrow, same time? John asked.

"Of course, will call you tomorrow," Mike added.

4

THE PROHIBITED TRANSACTIONS RULES

"I KNOW WE haven't really spent a lot of time discussing the types of investments you can make with a self-directed IRA; but I believe I mentioned that real estate, precious metals, hard-money lending, private business, tax liens/deeds, options, and private equity/hedge fund/venture capital tend to be the most popular types of self-directed IRA investments currently," John said.

"Yes—you did reference on an earlier call that self-directed IRA investors are making these types of investments," Mike said.

"Good. Before I jump into the prohibited transaction rules, I just want to make it clear that if you or your wife continued to invest your IRA or 401(k) plan funds into stocks and mutual funds, you would not have to worry about the prohibited transaction I am about to describe." John explained.

"That is what I thought," Mike responded, "because we have been investing our IRA funds for twenty-something years in traditional equities, and I have never heard of anything called the prohibited transaction rules."

THE BASICS OF PROHIBITED TRANSACTIONS

"Even though it sounds daunting," John said, "it's really not. But it is a little fuzzy. The IRC doesn't describe what a self-directed IRA or retirement plan can invest in, only what it *cannot* invest in. Specifically, IRC Sections 408 and 4975 prohibit disqualified persons from engaging in certain types of transactions. The purpose of these rules is to encourage the use of IRAs for the accumulation of retirement savings and to prohibit those in control of retirement plans from taking advantage of the tax benefits for their personal accounts."

"So it's sort of protecting my account from me?" Mike asked.

"In a way. Prohibited-transaction rules are based on the premise that investments involving retirement accounts and related parties should be handled in a way that benefits the retirement account and not the retirement-account owner."

"Would the IRS–prohibited transaction rules be different if I used a 401(k) retirement plan versus an IRA?" Mike asked.

"Not really. The main difference is that a 401(k) plan is able to purchase life-insurance contracts but an IRA is not," John clarified.

"So, if no harm would be coming to anyone except me, by my own hand, why should the IRS be so concerned about investments involving my retirement account and my family members?" Mike asked.

"Basically," John answered, "that's the only way the IRS can protect its very important revenue-generating distribution rules. It needs to make sure that if people want to use their retirement funds for personal purposes, that they pay tax and a penalty if they are under the age of 59½. In other words, it's the IRS's position that if you want to use retirement funds for personal purposes, that's OK as long as you pay the appropriate tax and penalty."

"Fair enough, I guess," Mike said. "I'd want to protect my revenue too."

"Exactly," John said. "So, in developing the disqualified-person rules, the IRS is basically saying that it believes a retirement-account holder and his or her lineal descendants are one and the same, and if retirement-account funds are being transferred directly or indirectly to a disqualified person, it is the same as if the retirement-account holder himself or herself were personally benefiting."

"That position makes sense," Mike said.

John nodded. "Yes. If you think about it—by giving money to your parents or children, you are clearly benefiting to some degree because of the close family relationship. For example, using your retirement account to pay your children's tuition or your parents' mortgage is either directly or indirectly benefiting you, because if your parents or kids benefit, you are also benefiting to some degree. The IRS's position is that, if you were able to transact with a disqualified person and use retirement-account funds, you could simply transfer the retirement-account funds to a child or parent and that would be just like him or her taking the money personally, which would eliminate the need to take a taxable distribution. This is something the IRS would definitely not appreciate."

"I think I get it," Mike said. "So if I could take some of my retirement-account funds and give them to my wife and kids, it would be pretty much the same as if I got to use the money personally."

"Right," John said. "The IRS was concerned that if they allowed this, people would be able to circumvent the distribution rules and avoid paying tax on their IRA accounts while simultaneously receiving some degree of benefit from the funds because they were used to help a close family member, such as a parent, child, or spouse."

"Ah, because I wouldn't have paid tax on that money otherwise, and I would still get to use it for my personal benefit."

"Remember," added John, "that in the case of a traditional pretax IRA or 401(k) plan, you were granted a tax deduction for the IRA or 401(k) plan contribution on the expectation that you would eventually pay tax on the accumulated pretax retirement account value. If you were able to take the pretax retirement funds and give them to a parent, spouse, or child, it would be like you were gaining use of the retirement funds without having to pay any tax or the 10 percent penalty, if applicable."

"And if that were possible, everyone would do it to avoid paying some taxes on that money," Mike said.

"Sure," John said. "And the IRS would be left with very little tax revenue from the pretax retirement account, and it would also lose tax revenue because of the use of the IRS deduction in the year of contribution—a double whammy."

"So prohibited-transaction rules are actually very important for the IRS," Mike said.

"The bottom line," John said, "is that most Americans' largest asset by the time they retire is their retirement account. The self-directed IRA and Solo 401(k) structure has become so popular over the last several years because the 2008 financial crisis hit those retirement assets so hard and showed people how important it is to diversify their retirement investments. The IRS has actually granted retirement investors a wide array of investment options when using retirement funds, but there are a number of important rules the IRS has codified that govern how IRA retirement funds are to be used."

"But like you said," Mike added, "the tricky part is that the IRS doesn't tell you what you can invest in or how you should use your IRA assets; it only tells you what you can't invest in or how you can't use those assets."

"Exactly," John said. "So prohibited transactions are important to follow if you want to gain maximum advantage from the work you are doing to create and grow your IRA retirement assets."

"Are the penalties for violating prohibited-transaction rules harsh enough to be worth worrying about?" Mike asked.

"Yes," John said, "they're steep. And if your IRA is your most valuable asset, as it is for most Americans, it will trigger a hefty tax and penalty with significant financial ramifications to your retirement."

"Are the prohibited-transaction rules the same for both traditional and Roth IRAs?" Mike asked.

John nodded. "The same rules apply to all IRAs, including traditional IRAs, Roth IRAs, SEP IRAs, and SIMPLE IRAs."

"I wonder why I never heard of prohibited-transaction rules before we started talking."

"You're not alone," John said. "Most Americans have never heard of the prohibited-transaction rules for good reason. After all, most retirement investors use their retirement funds to buy traditional financial assets, such as stocks, mutual funds, and exchange-traded funds (ETFs). With those investments, the chance of engaging in a prohibited transaction is slim to none. Hence, for people who are not interested in using retirement funds to make alternative-asset investments, the prohibited transaction rules are not extremely relevant; although, I think they are worth knowing about. For people who are interested in making alternative-asset investments with their retirement accounts, such as in real estate, the prohibited-transaction rules become very important. The good news is that the harsh penalties are easily avoidable. As long as you stay away from breaking the rules, you have no reason to fear the IRS when making self-directed IRA investments."

"OK," Mike said. "So what areas do we need to discuss?"

"Let's look at prohibited transactions that are restricted, because they pertain to disqualified persons, conflicts of interest, and self-dealing," John said. "And we should also look at exceptions and exemptions to the restrictions, as well as certain categories of transactions that are not allowed with a retirement account, such as the purchase of collectibles. Though there are many different scenarios stipulated in IRC Section 4975, and extensive case law clarifying those scenarios, the restrictions themselves are not complicated, and I can simplify them as much as possible to make them easier to follow. Even so, it can be helpful to get advice from a tax professional just to make sure you're on the straight-and-narrow path." John responded

DISQUALIFIED PERSONS

If a retirement-account transaction is restricted, it is likely because it pertains to a disqualified person. Who does the IRS consider a disqualified person?

Generally, this is referring to *you* (the IRA holder or 401(k) plan participant) and most of *your immediate family*, including your direct lineal ancestors or descendants as well as *any business* entities that hold a controlling equity or management interest in your retirement account.

Specifically, a disqualified person is

a. *you*, as the retirement-account holder, or any person with authority for making retirement-account investments;
b. *a trustee or custodian*, or a person providing services to the retirement account;
c. *the owner*—this is generally not applicable to IRAs and only really covers 401(k) plans;

d. *an employee organization*—this is generally not applicable to IRAs and only really covers 401(k) plans;

e. *a 50 percent owner* of (c) or (d);

f. *a family member* of (a), (b), (c), or (d), which includes your spouse, your parents and grandparents, your children and grandchildren, and their spouses, but not brothers, sisters, aunts, uncles, cousins, step-siblings, or friends;

g. *a partnership, corporation, trust, or estate* more than 50 percent owned or controlled by (a), (b), (c), (d), or (e);

h. *a 10 percent owner, officer, director, or highly compensated employee* of (c), (d), (e), or (g); or

i. *a 10 percent or more partner or joint venture* of (c), (d), (e), or (g).

In order to determine whether a proposed transaction is a prohibited transaction and violates IRC Section 4975, it is important to examine all the parties engaged in the proposed transaction rather than just the retirement-account owner.

According to IRC Section 4975, a retirement account is prohibited from engaging in certain types of transactions. The types of prohibited transactions can best be understood by dividing them into three categories: (1) direct pro-hibited transactions, (2) self-dealing prohibited transactions, and (3) conflict-of-interest prohibited transactions.

DIRECT OR INDIRECT PROHIBITED TRANSACTIONS

What is a direct or indirect prohibited transaction? Essentially, it is a transac-tion between the retirement account and a disqualified person, which either directly or indirectly personally benefits that disqualified person. It is im-portant to remember that the IRS–prohibited transaction rules are primar-ily in place to ensure that the use of retirement funds is in no way directly or indirectly personally benefiting the plan participant or any of his or her lineal descendants. The reason is clear. The IRS holds that if you wish to make personal use of your retirement funds to help yourself or a close family member, doing so is essentially like helping yourself. Accordingly, you must take a distribution and pay the tax and penalty if you are under 59½ years old. Those prohibited-transaction rules are basically the way the IRS polices and protects its distribution rules—a significant revenue source for the IRS and the US Treasury. In addition, when it comes to accumulating 401(k) and IRA funds, most of the funds are in pretax form, meaning the IRS provided the 401(k) plan participant or IRA holder with a tax deduction with the anticipation that the benefit provided to the taxpayer would be paid back in the form of taxation on the appreciated assets of the retirement account at a later time. It makes sense, then, that the IRS is so concerned with making sure that retirement funds are not used for any personal purpose that would allow someone to circumvent the distribution rules and taxation on the funds used. The IRS and Department of Labor need to protect their distribution rules, because that is how they ensure the IRS and US Treasury will receive the taxes they believe they deserve from retirement distributions.

Direct and indirect prohibited transactions are different. A direct prohibited transaction is the simplest type of prohibited transaction to uncover because it deals with scenarios involving a disqualified person and the retirement account directly. In contrast, an indirect prohibited transaction concerns transactions that do not appear to directly benefit a disqualified person but could do so indirectly based on certain facts and circumstances. For example, using your self-directed IRA to pay your personal credit-card bill would be a clear direct prohibited transaction. However, using your self-directed IRA to invest in a company of which you own 15 percent might be considered an indirect prohibited transaction based on certain facts and circumstances.

For example, you cannot use your retirement account to do the following with a disqualified person:

- Sell, exchange, or lease property
- Lend money or extend credit
- Furnish goods, services, or facilities
- Transfer income or assets

John told Mike that he was going to e-mail him a copy of IRC Section 4975 for his review. "Here are some scenarios pertaining to IRC Section 4975(c)(1)(A) that illustrate prohibited transactions to do with directly or indirectly selling, exchanging, or leasing property to a disqualified person."

IRC Section 4975(c)(1)(A): The direct or indirect sale, exchange, or leasing of property between a retirement account and a disqualified person

- Joe sells an interest in a piece of property owned by his retirement account to his son—PROHIBITED
- Beth leases real estate owned by her retirement account to her daughter—PROHIBITED
- Mark uses his retirement-account funds to purchase an LLC interest owned by his mother—PROHIBITED
- David uses his retirement-account funds to purchase an interest in an entity owned by his father—PROHIBITED
- Ted transfers property he owns personally, subject to a mortgage to his retirement account—PROHIBITED

The following are transactions to do with directly or indirectly lending money or extending credit to a disqualified person:

IRC Section 4975(c)(1)(B): The direct or indirect lending of money or other extension of credit between a retirement account and a disqualified person

- Ted lends his wife $70,000 from his retirement account—PROHIBITED
- Mary personally guarantees a bank loan to her retirement account to purchase real estate—PROHIBITED
- Ken lends his son $4,000 from his retirement account—PROHIBITED
- Chuck uses retirement-account funds to lend an entity owned and controlled by his father $45,000—PROHIBITED
- Eric acquires a credit card for his retirement account—PROHIBITED

John added, "There is an actual case I want to mention that I think demonstrates how IRC Section 4975(c)(1)(B) works."

"Please explain," Mike added.

"The case is called *Lawrence F. Peek, et ux., et al. v. Commissioner*, 140 TC 216 (5/9/2013). In this case, the court held that Mr. Peek, his attorney, and business colleague's personal guaranties of a loan/note from their newly formed corporation stock, of which was owned by taxpayers' self-directed IRA as part of an asset purchase transaction, was an IRC Section 4975 prohibited transaction. The court held that the fact that loan guaranties didn't involve IRAs directly was irrelevant since IRC Section 4975 was broadly worded to include both direct and indirect loans or guaranties to IRAs, by way of entities that IRAs owned." John added.

"Can you tell me more about the facts of the case," Mike said.

"Yes. In 2001, two taxpayers, Mr. Lawrence Peek and Darrel Fleck, sought to use self-directed IRAs to acquire a business. The taxpayers established self-directed IRAs using 401(k) rollovers, created a new company (FP Company), and then directed the IRAs to purchase the common stock of FP Company with the cash in the IRAs. FP Company then sought to purchase the business. To consummate the purchase, in addition to the cash and other credit lines, FP Company provided a promissory note to the sellers. This promissory note was backed by the personal guarantee of the taxpayers, and the guarantees were then backed by the deeds to the taxpayers' homes. The IRS audited the income tax return for both Mr. Peek and Mr. Fleck for the tax years of 2006 and 2007. Both Mr. Peek and Fleck contested the IRS's adjustment and filed a petition with the Tax Court. The IRS argued that Mr. Fleck and Mr. Peek's personal guarantee of a $200,000 promissory note from FP Company to the sellers of the business in 2001 as part of FP Company's purchase of the business assets were prohibited transactions. The Tax Court agreed with the IRS and found that the taxpayers had committed prohibited transactions, that the IRAs had ceased to be IRAs as of the beginning of 2001, and that the capital gain from the sale of FP Company by the IRAs was immediately taxed to the taxpayers. The Tax Court agreed with the IRS and held that since Internal Revenue Code Section 4975 prohibits both 'direct and indirect...lending of money or extensions of credit' between an IRA and its owner, it did not matter that the loan guarantee by the taxpayers was to FP Company and not the IRAs directly. Internal Revenue Code Section 4975 clearly prohibits the lending of money or extension of credit between a retirement plan and a disqualified person," John said.

"Very interesting case," Mike observed. "Always nice to hear about real-life examples of how these prohibited transaction rules work."

"I agree. Let's now move on to examining IRC 4975(c)(1)(C)," John said.

IRC Section 4975(c)(1)(C): The direct or indirect furnishing of goods, services, or facilities between a retirement account and a disqualified person

- Andrew buys a piece of property with his retirement-account funds and hires his father to work on the property—PROHIBITED
- Rachel buys a condo with her retirement-account funds and personally fixes it up—PROHIBITED
- Bill purchases a condo with his retirement-account funds and paints the walls without receiving a fee—PROHIBITED
- Henry buys a piece of property with his retirement-account funds and hires his son to work on the property—PROHIBITED
- Mary buys a home with her retirement account, and her son makes repairs —PROHIBITED
- Matt acts as the real estate agent for his retirement account—PROHIBITED

INDIRECT PROHIBITED TRANSACTIONS

Indirect prohibited transactions inspire a lot of debate because the determination of whether a prohibited transaction occurs is largely based on the facts and circumstances.

Indirect prohibited transactions are transactions that may not violate any of the direct prohibited-transaction rules on their face, but still may be considered a prohibited transaction by the IRS. For example, when an individual uses a retirement account to invest in a company in which he or she owns a 15 percent share, this would not seem to be a prohibited transaction; this is because the individual retirement-account holder owns less than 50 percent of the entity, and the entity does not seem to be a disqualified person under IRC Section 4975. However, if it turns out that the company needed the funds to avoid bankruptcy or the investment was made to secure a job within the company, the IRS could argue that the investment directly or indirectly helped the retirement-account holder personally.

Many tax professionals fail to focus on the indirect prohibited-transaction rules outlined in IRC Section 4975 and just focus on the direct prohibited-transaction rules. The IRS seems to be using the indirect prohibited-transaction rules as a tool for scrutinizing retirement account transactions that seem to personally benefit the retirement-account holder but don't violate the direct prohibited-transaction rules under IRC Section 4975.

The following examples will help illustrate.

Subject to the exemptions under IRC Section 4975(d), an indirect prohibited transaction generally involves one of the following:

IRC Section 4975(c)(1)(D): The direct or indirect transfer to a disqualified person of income or assets of a retirement account

- Ken is in a financial jam and takes $32,000 from his retirement account to pay a personal debt—PROHIBITED
- John uses his retirement account to purchase a rental property and hires his friend to manage the property. The friend then enters into a contract with John and transfers those funds back to John—PROHIBITED
- Bryan purchases a vacation home with his retirement-account funds and stays in the home on occasion—PROHIBITED
- Elliot buys a cottage on the lake with her retirement-account funds and rents it out to her daughter and son-in-law—PROHIBITED
- Larry uses his retirement-account funds to purchase real estate and earns a commission as the real estate agent on the sale—PROHIBITED

John added, "I have another real-life case that I think really helps us understand how IRC Section 4975(c)(1)(D) and the self-dealing prohibited transactions I will soon discuss work. The case is *Ellis v. Comm.*, cited as 115 AFTR 2d 2015-2072 (787 F.3d 1213), Code Sec(s) 4975; 408; 72; 61; 72; 7491, (CA8), 06/05/2015. In *Ellis*, the Tax Court held that that Mr. Ellis/general manager of a used car business/LLC, which was held 98 percent by IRA, engaged in a prohibited transaction under IRC Section 4975 when he caused the corporation ("CST") to pay him compensation. The court held that Mr. Ellis, as the IRA's fiduciary and beneficial shareholder, engaged in indirect transfer of the IRA's income and assets for his own benefit, in violation of IRC Section 4975(c)(1)(D), and indirectly dealt with such income and assets for his own interest or his own account, in violation of IRC Section 4975(c)(1)(E). The Ellis court argued that the Tax Court erred in upholding the commissioner's determination that Mr. Ellis engaged in a prohibited transaction by causing CST to pay him wages. The court agreed with the Tax Court, which held that Mr. Ellis engaged in a prohibited transaction by directing the company, 98 percent owned by the IRA, to pay him a salary. The record establishes that Mr. Ellis caused his IRA to invest a substantial majority of its value in CST with the understanding that he would receive compensation for his services as general manager. By directing CST to pay him wages from funds that the company received almost exclusively from his IRA, Mr. Ellis engaged in the indirect transfer of the income and assets of the IRA for his own benefit and indirectly dealt with such income and assets for his own interest or his own account (IRC Section 4975(c)(1)(D) & (E)," John explained.

"The case seems pretty straightforward. Don't invest your IRA funds in a closely held entity in which you or a disqualified person will be compensated, especially if the IRA will own more than 50 percent," Mike deduced.

"Yes—exactly," responded John. "But the interesting thing about Ellis is that, if he would have used an IRA instead of a 401(k) plan, he could have availed himself of a prohibited transaction exemption under IRC 4975(d)(13), which involves the purchase of qualifying employer securities, also known as the rollover business start-up solution, or ROBS. I will be discussing some of the prohibited transaction exemptions shortly. But before that, I want to talk more about the self-dealing prohibited transactions."

SELF-DEALING PROHIBITED TRANSACTIONS

"Self-dealing," John explained, "is a term for a situation that arises when someone benefits on both sides of a deal. According to IRC Section 4975(c)(1)(E), self-dealing, which is a form of an indirect prohibited transaction, occurs when you directly or indirectly use the income or assets of your retirement account to further your own interests or benefit your own accounts."

IRC Section 4975(c)(1)(E): The direct or indirect act by a disqualified person who is a fiduciary whereby he/she deals with income or assets of the retirement account in his or her own interest or for his or her own account

- Debra, who is a real estate agent, uses her retirement-account funds to buy a piece of property *and* earns a commission from the sale—PROHIBITED
- Karen makes an investment, using her retirement-account funds, into a company she controls that will benefit her personally—PROHIBITED
- Brett uses his retirement-account funds to invest in a partnership with himself personally in which he and his family will own more than 50 percent of the partnership—PROHIBITED
- Rick uses his retirement-account funds to lend money to a business that he controls and manages—PROHIBITED
- Helen uses her retirement-account funds to invest in a real estate fund managed by her son, who receives a bonus for securing her investment—PROHIBITED
- Warren uses his retirement-account funds to invest in his son's business, which is in financial trouble—PROHIBITED

REAL-LIFE EXAMPLES

John went on by saying, "Here's a real-life example of a self-dealing prohibited transaction.

ROLLINS V. COMMISSIONER, T.C. MEMO 2004-60

Rollins v. Commissioner is an important case because it illustrates how one can engage in a prohibited transaction with an entity even if the entity is not a disqualified entity per se. The *Rollins* case also is important for examining whether a potential transaction could be considered an indirect prohibited transaction under IRC Section 4975." John said,

John continued, "the facts in *Rollins* are as follows: Mr. Rollins owned his own CPA firm. He was sole trustee of its 401(k) plan. Mr. Rollins caused his plan to lend funds to three companies in which he was the largest stockholder (9 percent to 33 percent), but not controlling stockholder. The companies had twenty-eight, seventy, and eighty other stockholders, respectively. Mr. Rollins made the decision for the companies to borrow from his 401(k) plan. The loans were demand loans, secured by each company's assets. The interest rate was market rate or higher. Mr. Rollins signed loan checks for his plan and signed notes for borrowers. All loans were repaid in full.

Mr. Rollins acknowledged that he was a disqualified person with regard to the plan because he owns Rollins, the CPA firm, but he contends that: (1) none of the corporations that were the borrowers was a disqualified person, (2) none of the loans were transactions between him and the plan, and (3) he "did not benefit from these loans, either in income or in his own account." John said.

"I am curious how the Tax Court ruled," Mike said.

" The Tax Court held that IRC Section 4975(c)(1)(D), indirect prohibition, did not require an actual transfer of money or property between the plan and the disqualified person. The fact that a disqualified person could have benefited as a result of the use of plan assets was sufficient. The Tax Court held that the transactions were used by Rollins or for his benefit and were assets of the plan. These assets of the plan were not transferred to Rollins. For each of those transactions, however, Rollins sat on both sides of the table.

Rollins made the decisions to lend the plan's funds, and Rollins signed the promissory notes on behalf of the borrowers. One of the more interesting parts of the *Rollins* case was the Tax Court's emphasis that, as the taxpayer, the burden of proof is the responsibility of the taxpayer. In other words, at its core, the Rollins case is a burden-of-proof case that illustrates the breadth of the application of IRC Section 4975(c)(1)(D) as well as the difficulty of meeting that burden of proof. Mr. Rollins was not a majority owner of any of the borrowers, but he was the largest shareholder for each company. And he also signed the notes for each borrower. John said.

"Would the same decision have been made if Mr. Rollins was not the largest shareholder or had not, as the court put it, "sat on both sides of the table" (e.g., by not signing the notes on behalf of the borrowers)?" Mike asked

"It's not entirely clear if that would have influenced the court since it was still Mr. Rollins's burden (as the disqualified person) to prove that the transaction did not enhance or was not intended to enhance the value of his investments in the borrowers. That seems to be a very tough burden to meet. Moreover, as the court noted, the fact that a transaction is a good investment for the plan has nothing to do with the problem. The lesson is that caution should be exercised whenever a disqualified person is sitting "on both sides of the table," John concluded.

"Let's now move into looking at the conflict-of-interest prohibited transactions," John said.

CONFLICT-OF-INTEREST PROHIBITED TRANSACTIONS

"According to IRC 4975(c)(i)(F), a prohibited transaction also occurs when a disqualified person is connected to a transaction involving the income or assets of the retirement account. This is called a conflict-of-interest prohibited transaction. For example:

IRC Section 4975(c)(i)(F): Receipt of any consideration by a disqualified person who is a fiduciary for his or her own account from any party

dealing with the retirement account in connection with a transaction involving income or assets of the retirement account:

- Jason uses his retirement-account funds to loan money to a company that he manages and controls and also owns a small ownership interest in—PROHIBITED
- Cathy uses her retirement account to lend money to a business that she works for in order to secure a promotion—PROHIBITED
- Eric uses his retirement-account funds to invest in a fund that he manages and where his management fee is based on the total value of the fund's assets—PROHIBITED," John said.

"Can I partner with myself to do a self-directed IRA real estate investment? Mike asked.

"That's one of the most popular questions I get from prospective real estate investors seeking to use retirement funds to make real estate investments," John said. "'Can I use some personal funds to co-invest with my self-directed IRA funds?' The majority of Americans have anywhere between $65,000 and $150,000 in a retirement account. A single-family home could easily exceed the amount of retirement funds held by that individual. With most banks not overly eager to make real estate–related loans, especially nonrecourse loans, using personal funds along with your retirement funds to make an investment is very appealing. The problem with comingling retirement and personal funds to make an investment is that the IRS could argue that the transaction violates the IRS self-dealing and conflict of interest prohibited transactions pursuant to IRC Sections 4975(c)(1)(D),(E), and (F). The IRS could easily make the case that using retirement funds to make a real estate investment personally benefitted the individual because, without the retirement funds, the real estate investment could not have been made personally. However, there is a recent case that I think sheds some light as to how the IRS feels about a disqualified person using personal and retirement funds in the same real estate transaction," John said.

"What is the case called?" Mike asked.

"IN RE: KELLERMAN, Cite as 115 AFTR 2d 2015-1944 (531 B.R. 219), Code Sec(s) 408; 4975, (Bktcy Ct AR), 05/26/2015, offers some good insight into the potential risk of partnering with your self-directed IRA. "The *Kellerman* case involved a construction company owner and wife/LLC co-owners (the Kellermans) who were denied a claim for bankruptcy estate exemption for Mr. Kellerman's self-directed IRA. The court concluded that Mr. Kellerman, along with his wife, engaged in prohibited transactions by directing the IRA to deliver property as noncash contribution to the IRA and LLC and to make cash contribution to the partnership to develop property. The Kellermans filed their voluntary Chapter 11 bankruptcy petition in the United States Bankruptcy Court. Prior to his bankruptcy case, Barry Kellerman created the IRA, which, as of October 27, 2008, had a reported value of $252,112.67. The named administrator of the IRA was Entrust Mid South, LLC ("Entrust"). The IRA was self-directed by Barry Kellerman, who made all the decisions pertinent to the issues raised in the objections. At the commencement of their case, the debtors valued the IRA at $180,000 and claimed the entire fund as exempt under the Bankruptcy Act. The alleged prohibited transactions involved the 2007 acquisition of approximately four acres of real property located near Maumelle, Arkansas. Panther Mountain Land Development, LLC ("Panther Mountain") played a precipitating and integral role in the purchase. Barry Kellerman and his wife each owned a 50 percent interest in Panther Mountain. To effect the acquisition and development of the four-acre property, the IRA and Panther Mountain formed a partnership whereby the IRA contributed property and Panther Mountain contributed property and cash. The purchase of the four-acre tract also took place on August 8, 2007. Barry Kellerman made the decision to purchase the four acres. The purchase took place principally to complement and assist in the development of two nearby tracts of approximately 80 and 120 acres owned by Panther Mountain. While the four-acre tract could be independently developed, controlling it substantially assisted in the development of the other Panther Mountain properties. The IRA funded the entire purchase price. The court concluded that, in 2007, Barry Kellerman engaged the IRA in transactions, including: (1) the purchase of the real property with IRA funds and subsequent conveyance of the real property to the IRA and Panther Mountain (the "noncash contribution" under the Partnership Agreement), and (2) the cash contribution of $40,523.93 made by the IRA to the Entrust Partnership (the "cash contribution" under the Partnership Agreement). Collectively, individually, and with some redundancy, both the noncash contribution and the cash contribution constituted "prohibited transactions" with disqualified persons pursuant to IRC Sections 4975(c)(1)(B), (D), and (E), which rendered the IRA nonexempt," John expounded.

"Interesting," Mike said. "I have heard from some of my friends that their IRA custodians allowed them to use personal and retirement funds in the same real estate transaction, but based on this case that seems somewhat risky."

"Yes," answered John. "I would agree. I believe this case is a clear example that using retirement and personal funds in the same transaction can potentially trigger a self-dealing prohibited transaction under IRC 4975(c)(1)(D). By entering into a transaction with IRA funds that in some way directly or indirectly involves a disqualified person, in this case Panther Mountain, the IRA owner then is saddled with the burden of proving the transaction does not violate any of the self-dealing or conflict of interest prohibited transaction rules under IRC Section 4975, a burden that, as this case shows, could be difficult to satisfy. As the court stated…"

"Further, and cumulatively, Barry Kellerman transferred or used 'the income or assets of [the IRA]' for the benefit of each of the aforementioned disqualified persons and as a fiduciary dealt with 'the income or assets of [the IRA] in his own interest or for his own account.' IRC Section 4975(c)(1)(D),(E). Barry Kellerman, as the owner and fiduciary of the IRA, (1) orchestrated the IRA's membership in the Entrust Partnership with Panther Mountain, (2) signed the Buy Direction Letter and the Sale Letter that facilitated the purchase of the four acres solely by the IRA but held with Panther Mountain as tenants in common, and (3) directed the payment of "Business Expense[s]" by the IRA to develop the four-acre tract. The real purpose for these transactions was to directly benefit Panther Mountain and the Kellermans in developing both the four acres and the contiguous properties owned by Panther Mountain. The Kellermans each own a 50 percent interest in Panther Mountain and stood to benefit substantially if the four-acre tract and the adjoining land were developed into a residential subdivision."

John added: "The Kellerman case is a great example why using retirement funds and personal assets in the same transaction is not advisable as it can potentially trigger the IRC Section 4975 prohibited transaction rules."

"Got it. Very helpful," Mike responded.

"Just like the Kellerman case," John continued, "the IRS could also argue that using retirement and personal funds in the same real estate transaction could be considered the transfer or use by or for the benefit of a disqualified person of the income or assets of a plan. The analysis generally depends on the facts and circumstances involved in the transaction at issue but, anytime personal and retirement funds are used together in one investment, the door is open for the IRS to argue a prohibited transaction occurred. With the burden on the taxpayer for proving a prohibited transaction did not occur, I always advise not to use any personal funds in connection with an investment involving retirement funds."

"What if I have enough in my self-directed IRA to make the investment but I still think it's a good investment for my self-directed IRA and personal funds?"

"That's another question I get often," John said. "The scenario is typically as follows: You are looking to buy a property and can make the investment personally or via your retirement account, since both include ample funds. But you want to own the property through some shared percentage of retirement account and personal funds."

"Is that permitted?" Mike asked.

"The problem is that any time retirement funds and personal funds are mixed in an investment, there's no guarantee that the IRS could not try to argue that it's a self-dealing or conflict of interest prohibited transaction pursuant to IRC Section 4975, as we saw in the Kellerman case. With the burden of proof falling on the taxpayer to prove otherwise, and with that burden of proof being difficult to meet, it's best practice to stay away from using a combination of personal and retirement funds in a single real estate transaction. All in all, I suggest never commingling self-directed IRA and personal funds in one transaction. I think it's highly risky, and it opens the door for the IRS to argue a prohibited transaction has occurred. You'll see why when I go over the prohibited transaction rules. The repercussions can be very steep and painful," John said.

"OK—but what types of services, if any, can a real estate investor provide to the self-directed IRA real estate investment?" Mike asked.

"This is probably one of the most-asked questions I receive from real estate investors looking to use a self-directed IRA to purchase real estate. Up until 2014, there was not much case law on this subject," John explained.

"So what case changed this?" Mike asked.

John related the details of the case: "IN RE: CHERWENKA, Cite as 113 AFTR 2d 2014-2333 (508 B.R. 228), Code Sec(s) 408; 4975, (Bktcy Ct GA), 03/06/2014. The *Cherwenka* case involved a Georgia statutory bankruptcy estate exemption for an individual retirement account within the meaning of IRC Section 408, covering self-directed IRAs held by Michael Cherwenka, who was in business of 'flipping houses.' Contrary to the creditor claim that the IRA lost its IRC Section 408 qualification when the taxpayer engaged in prohibited transactions under IRC Section 4975 by co-owning property with the IRA, the court held there was no evidence of any such prohibited ownership structure for the stated property or that the taxpayer impermissibly benefited from the apportioned purchase and resale of same. In this case, Michael Cherwenka established a self-directed IRA with Pensco to buy real estate. After a property was purchased, the property was resold. Any and all profits from the sale of any Pensco IRA asset are realized exclusively by the Pensco IRA. Sometimes the properties would be renovated or improved before sale. Sometimes the properties would simply be held and sold at a later date, hopefully capitalizing on advantageous market conditions or market swings. It is unclear whether the decision to improve a property and to what extent the properties were improved was made by Cherwenka or a contractor he regularly engaged. Cherwenka was not compensated for any real property research he performed, nor was he compensated for any recommendations, management, or consulting services he provided relating to how the Pensco IRA properties were improved before resale. Cherwenka explained his role in the buying and selling of these properties as being limited to identifying the asset for purchase and later selling the asset. Cherwenka then would engage his contractors to decide on or oversee the scope of work with improved properties. Cherwenka testified that he "read and approved" the expense forms prior to Pensco paying funds to reimburse the submitted expenses. Contractors were paid by the job, which accounted for labor costs, but no management fee or additional cost was included in the expenses submitted to Pensco. Cherwenka stated he would inspect or confirm that work was completed through site visits or communication with his 'team' before he would approve expenses to be paid by Pensco. Of interest, Cherwenka stated that he had never jointly owned a property with Pensco. Yet, he also testified that the property was owned in part by Pensco and in part by him personally. The debtor recollected that he owned 55 percent of the property with the remaining 45 percent owned by the Pensco IRA."

"So he actually did own the property personally with his IRA, but the creditors never actually were able to prove that?" Mike asked.

"Yes—pretty much, and who knows if the court would have ruled against Cherwenka if that fact was proven. In any event, the case offers some great insight as to the types of activities allowed to be performed when a self-directed IRA invests in real estate. In *Cherwenka*, it was argued that Cherwenka performed work on the properties by researching and identifying the subject properties, appointing and approving work on the properties, and overseeing payment from Pensco for such work, and that those acts constitute prohibited transactions under IRC Section 4975(c)(1)(C) as direct and indirect services by the IRA holder, a disqualified person. The court disagreed and held that the state's position requires the court to read out of the statute the word 'transaction.' There is no evidence that Cherwenka engaged in any transaction. A transaction includes an exchange of goods or services, and the evidentiary record does not include that Cherwenka received anything in exchange for his alleged services. In fact, Cherwenka's testimony included that he received no money, discount, or other benefit for the identified activities he undertook with the Pensco IRA. Although Cherwenka was a disqualified person based on his ownership of the IRA, the court found that the debtor's involvement in selecting property and participating in other actions taken by the IRA did not constitute a prohibited transaction because the evidence failed to demonstrate that the IRA-owned properties resulted in any benefit to Cherwenka outside of the plan," John said.

"That is really interesting. Is there any specific language in the case that sets forth what can and can't be done by a disqualified person in terms of activities or tasks relating to the self-directed IRA?" Mike asked.

"Actually, the court said the following: 'Self-directed IRAs are authorized by federal law and are held by a trustee or custodian that permits investment in a broader set of assets than is permitted by traditional IRA custodians.' *Levine v. Entrust Grp., Inc.*, 2012 WL 6087399 (N.D. Cal. Dec. 6, 2012). By its very nature, the debtor, as IRA owner, is required to make decisions regarding the Pensco IRA's assets and investments. Essentially, debtor's decision-making regarding asset acquisition and sale is characterized by the state as a prohibited transaction under IRC 4975(c)(1)(C)—as a service between a plan (Pensco IRA) and a disqualified person (Cherwenka). However, the recognition of self-directed IRAs as qualified IRAs necessarily implies that a disqualified person (the owner as fiduciary) will make investment decisions regarding the plan. The State has failed to establish sufficient evidence that Cherwenka received any personal benefit besides asset appreciation of those properties held by the Pensco IRA. There is no evidence to support a determination that Cherwenka's selection of real estate and any other decisions or recommendations regarding the IRA-owned properties resulted in any benefit to Cherwenka outside of the plan. There is no basis to hold that Cherwenka's actions constituted a prohibited transaction, so there is no basis to disqualify the Pensco IRA," John expanded.

"That is a really helpful case for any real estate investor looking into the type of activities or tasks he or she can perform as the IRA owner with respect to the self-directed IRA real estate investment," Mike said.

"I agree. The Cherwenka case is an important case in the self-directed IRA real estate context, because it appears to hold that engaging in passive activities related to the purchase and sale of real estate assets would not rise to the level of a transaction involving goods and services pursuant to IRC 4975 and, thus, trigger the prohibited transaction rules. In this case, Cherwenka would locate the real estate to serve as the investment for the self-directed Pensco IRA. A real estate agent would then work with him to submit a proposed offer to Pensco. Cherwenka would then review the closing statements and communicate with Pensco in instances where there were discrepancies in fees or other figures on the HUD-1 or related documents. Cherwenka was not compensated for any real property research he performed, nor was he compensated for any recommendation, management, or consulting services he provided relating to how the Pensco IRA properties were improved before resale. Cherwenka explained his role in the buying and selling of these properties as being limited to identifying the asset for purchase and later selling the asset. Cherwenka engaged contractors to decide or oversee the scope of work with improved properties. Cherwenka testified that he 'read and approved' the expense forms prior to Pensco paying funds to reimburse the submitted expenses. Contractors were paid by the job, which accounted for labor costs, but no management fee or additional cost was included in the expenses submitted to Pensco. Cherwenka stated he would inspect or confirm that work was completed through site visits or communication with his "'team' before he would approve expenses to be paid by Pensco. In essence, the case gives real estate investors a good road map or guide as to the types of activities that would likely not be considered transactions or services under the prohibited transaction rules pursuant to IRC Section 4975. Because most real estate investors tend to perform the same sorts of tasks that Cherwenka performed, the case offers a legal foundation for the position that passive real estate activities performed by the IRA holder in the context of a self-directed IRA real estate transaction would not be considered a prohibited transaction. Moreover, the fact that Cherwenka used his IRA and personal funds in the same transaction could have changed the court's ruling in the case that Cherwenka engaged in a prohibited transaction; however, the State, for some reason, was not able to prove the co-ownership. Like the Kellerman case showed (KELLERMAN, Cite as 115 AFTR 2d 2015-1944 (531 B.R. 219), Code Sec(s) 408; 4975, (Bktcy Ct AR), 05/26/2015), using retirement and personal funds in the same transaction is not advisable and could trigger a prohibited transaction under IRC 4975," John stated.

"That is really helpful. I will definitely be telling my friends who are using a self-directed IRA to buy and sell real estate about this case," Mike added.

"OK—let's move on to some of the exceptions around the prohibited transaction rules outlined in IRC 4975(c)," John said.

STATUTORY EXEMPTIONS TO THE PROHIBITED-TRANSACTION RULES

"There are a lot of situations to consider," Mike said.

"Yes," John responded. "Like I said, the IRS doesn't tell you what you can do, only what you can't, and that understanding develops like any tax law."

"But I don't need to be an expert and know everything," Mike said. "I just need to start by thinking about my particular situation or the investments I want to make."

"Exactly," John said. "And then check with a tax attorney or CPA who understands the IRS–prohibited transaction rules to make sure."

"The most popular way for satisfying a prohibited-transaction exemption is the statutory exemption, because anyone who complies with the terms of the statute will be able to benefit from the exemption."

John continued to explain:

"In IRC Section 4975(d), Congress created certain statutory exemptions from the prohibited transactions outlined in IRC Section 4975(c). These exemptions were established because Congress believed there was a legitimate reason to permit them, as long as certain specified requirements were satisfied. In such situations, Congress has decided to issue blanket prohibited-transaction exemptions permitting certain types of transactions, as long as certain requirements prescribed in the statute are met.

The most common prohibited-transaction exemption involves participant loans from a 401(k) plan. Unfortunately, the 401(k) plan loan feature does do not apply to IRAs. IRC Section 4975(d)(1) describes conditions under which loans are allowable. The majority of the statutory exemptions found under IRC Section 4975(d) are not commonly applied because of their specific application, such as the ability to invest plan assets in bank-deposit accounts where the bank is the employer, or to invest plan assets in life insurance–company products where the company is the employer. However, besides the 401(k) loan exemption, the other common prohibited-transaction exemption often used is IRC Section 4975(d)(13), which addresses the ability to use a 401(k) plan to buy corporation stock (qualifying employer securities), which is the basis for something called the Rollover Business Start-up Solution, or ROBS. Unfortunately, the exceptions to the prohibited-transaction rules are so narrow and limited in scope that most self-directed retirement-account investors are not able to take advantage of any of them when making self-directed IRA investments."

"That's what I figured," Mike said.

"Yes," John agreed. "Navigating IRS–prohibited transaction rules is complex and requires a thorough examination of the facts and circumstances involved in the retirement account transaction before determining whether a prohibited transaction has occurred. In fact, in addition to the prohibited-transaction rules under IRC Section 4975, the plan-asset rules is a set of rules that can trigger the prohibited-transaction rules. The plan-asset rules are generally designed to apply 'look-through' rules to interests held by a retirement account in an investment fund, such as a hedge fund. I don't want to get into too many details on the plan-asset rules because it mostly relates to investment funds, but I just wanted you to be aware of the broad scope of the prohibited-transaction rules."

"OK, I understand and definitely want to stay away from doing any type of transaction with my retirement accounts that could trigger a prohibited transaction," Mike said.

"Unfortunately, there are a number of other categories of investments that are not permitted to be made with retirement accounts," added John.

OTHER PROHIBITED ASSETS

"There are a number of other investments," John continued, "that are not permitted. These investments do not fall under the prohibited-transaction rules under IRC Section 4975 but are outlined under IRC Section 408. I talked about those in detail already. But just to review, a retirement account can't invest in collectibles such as

- any work of art;
- any metal or gem;
- any alcoholic beverage;
- any rug or antique;
- any stamp; and
- most coins."

"Right," Mike said, "I remember being surprised by that."

"Well," John explained, "the basic reason these types of assets are prohibited from being purchased with retirement funds is that they are generally hard to value and difficult to sell."

"Makes sense," Mike said.

"Remember, though, that .99 percent pure gold, silver, or platinum bullion, as well as American Eagle and state-minted coins, are approved investments for your retirement account and will not trigger a prohibited transaction."

"How do I take possession of precious metals or IRS-approved coins?" Mike asked.

"Great question. IRC Section 408(m) lists the types of precious metals and coins that are permitted investments using IRA funds:

(A) any coin which is—

(i.) a gold coin described in paragraph (7), (8), (9), or (10) of section 5112(a) of title 31, United States Code, (ii.) a silver coin described in section 5112(e) of title 31, United States Code,

(iii.) a platinum coin described in section 5112(k) of title 31, United States Code, or

(iv.) a coin issued under the laws of any State, or

(B) any gold, silver, platinum, or palladium bullion of a fineness equal to or exceeding the minimum fineness that a contract market (as described in section 7 of the Commodity Exchange Act, 7 U.S.C. 7) [2] requires for metals which may be delivered in satisfaction of a regulated futures contract, if such bullion is in the physical possession of a trustee described under subsection (a) of this section.

John continued, "In addition, the Technical and Miscellaneous Revenue Act of 1988 allowed IRA owners to invest in state minted coins so long as they are not held in the possession of the IRA holder. IRC Section 408(m)(3)(A) lists the type of coins that may be purchased with retirement funds, which generally are American Eagle and U.S. state minted coins of a certain finesse. Whereas, IRC 408(m)(3)(B), refers to gold, silver, or palladium bullion of a certain finesse which must be held in the physical possession of a U.S. trustee, as described under subsection IRC 408(a). A trustee is defined in IRC Section 408(a) as "a bank (as defined in subsection (n)) or such other person who demonstrates to the satisfaction of the Secretary that the manner in which such other person will administer the trust will be consistent with the requirements of this section." Internal Revenue Code Section 408(n) defines a bank as any bank (as defined in section 581) or an insured credit union (within the meaning of paragraph (6) or (7) of section 101 of the Federal Credit Union Act). Section 581 defines a bank as a bank or trust company incorporated and doing business under the laws of the United States (including laws relating to the District of Columbia) or of any State, a substantial part of the business of which consists of receiving deposits and making loans and discounts, or of exercising fiduciary powers similar to those permitted to national banks under authority of the Comptroller of the Currency, and which is subject by law to supervision and examination by State, Territorial, or Federal authority having supervision over banking institutions. Such term also means a domestic building and loan association. The Code seems to suggest that metals cannot be held in a foreign bank account since it would not satisfy the definition of a bank. " John said.

John continued, "The question then becomes what does "physical possession" mean and does the bank where the metals or coins are being held either physically or in a safe deposit box have to be the bank where the IRA was established or could it be any bank or financial institution that satisfies the definition of trustee under IRC Section 408." John said,

."Ok – I get it. So I should not Hold IRS approved coins or precious metals/bullion personally," Mike said.

"Correct. IRC Section 408(m) clearly states that gold, silver, or palladium bullion must be held in the physical possession of a trustee, otherwise known as a U.S. bank, financial institution or approved trust company. Hence, IRS approved precious metals may <u>not</u> be held personally or anywhere outside of the physical possession of a U.S. trustee, as defined under IRC Section 408(a)." John said.

"But what about IRS approved coins?" Mike asked.

"So the question is, can IRS approved coins, as described in IRC Section 408(m)(3)(A), be held personally? Unfortunately, there is not much IRS guidance on this point, but since coins may also be bullion, as defined in IRC Section 408(m)(3)(B), most tax practitioners take the position that IRS approved coins purchased by a retirement account should be held in the physical possession of a trustee, as defined under IRC Section 408. However, the Technical and Miscellaneous Revenue Act of 1988 does state that a retirement account may purchase state minted coins so long as a person holds them independent of the IRA owner. The 1988 Act does not define "Person" and interestingly does not refer to the term "trustee." So can one hold IRS approved coins personally? I believe that IRS approved coins should not be held personally by the IRA holder and should be held in the physical possession of a trustee, as defined in IRC Section 408. " John said.

"Very interesting. That begs the next question; can a self-directed IRA LLC hold IRS approved coins and precious metals/bullion in a safe deposit box in the name of the IRA LLC?" Mike asked.

"Ok. Let's start with coins. For a self-directed IRA LLC, IRS approved coins are purchased by the LLC manager in the name of the LLC, which is owned by the IRA. So where can the manager of the LLC hold the coins. Clearly, the safest approach, and the approach we recommend to all of our clients, is for the coins to be held in the physical possession of a trustee, as defined in Section 408, such as a depository. But what about a bank safe deposit box in the name of the IRA LLC. Again, there is no formal IRS guidance on this point, but here are a few points to consider:

John continued, "If a an IRA holder holds coins in a safe deposit box at a U.S. bank in the name of the self-directed IRA LLC the coins are clearly not being held by the IRA owner personally, which in the case of state minted coins would seem to satisfy the language in Technical and Miscellaneous Revenue Act of 1988. In the case of IRS approved coins that are not state minted, IRC Section 408(m) (3)(A) does not seemingly include a "physical possession" requirement, however, some IRS approved coins, such as American Eagles, can be considered bullion and could then fall under the "physical possession" requirement under IRC 408(m)(3) (B) for bullion. Thus, holding IRS approved coins at a bank safety deposit box in the name of the IRA LLC is certainly not in the physical possession of the IRA holder since they will physically be held in a safe deposit box of the bank in the name of the IRA LLC. However, the question, then becomes is the bank where the coins are being stored in the name of the LLC considered the trustee of the IRA, as defined by IRC Section 408. The definition of a U.S. trustee is outlined in IRC Section 408(a), which discusses the definition of an IRA. So the argument goes if the IRS approved coins are held at a bank safe deposit box in the name of the LLC and the bank is not the trustee or the custodian of the IRA that holds the coins, then is the physical possession definition satisfied and is the bank acting as the IRA trustee? There are arguments on both sides. For example, IRC Section 408(m) also applies to 401(k) plans and the definition of a 401(k) plan trustee is not the same as a trustee of an IRA. Since the physical possession requirement outlined in IRC Section 408(m)(3)(B) applies to IRAs and 401(k) plans, some tax practitioners believe that the definition is satisfied so long as the coins are held at a bank or financial institution that satisfies the definition of trustee, as outlined in IRC Section 408(m), and not necessarily the actual trustee of the retirement account. The language in IRC Section 408(m)(3)(B) uses the term "a" trustee" and not "the" trustee" offering some support for the position that the coins can be held at any trustee, as defined under IRC 408(a) and not just the trustee of the IRA. This would make sense since a depository is considered a trustee pursuant to IRC Section 408(a), but may not be the actual trustee of the IRA owning the coins." John said.

"OK. Very interesting. It seems like with IRS approved coins; a self-directed IRA investor could make some arguments for holding them with a third-party without holding the coins at a depository." Mike stated.

"Yes – but I would prefer that you hold the IRS approved coin with a trustee, as defined in IRC Section 408(s), such as a depository, even in the case of state minted coins. It is just much safer. Now let's turn to bullion/precious metals." John said.

"Ok – sounds good." Mike responded.

"In the case of IRS approved bullion, which may not apply to certain coins, does using a bank safety deposit box in the name of the IRA LLC satisfy the rules under IRC Section 408(m)? Unlike coins, IRC Section 408(m)(3)(B) clearly holds that the IRS approved bullion must be held in the physical possession of a trustee. We have learned that a trustee is defined under IRC Section 408 as a U.S bank, financial institution, or approved trust company, including a depository. If a an IRA holder holds IRS approved bullion, as defined under IRC Section 408(m)(3)(B) in a safe deposit box at a U.S. bank in the name of the Self-Directed IRA LLC is that considered to satisfy the definition of "physical possession" of a trustee, as defined in IRC Section 408. Well the argument goes that the precious metals/bullion are certainly not in the physical posses-sion of the IRA holder since they will physically be held in a safe deposit box of the bank. Although, an argument can be made that the safe deposit box is constructively in the control of the IRA holder, since he or she has the keys for the box. However, IRC Section 408 clearly states "physical possession" and not "constructive control". From a legal standpoint, possession is not defined to rep-resent control, meaning one can be in possession of an item but not in control or ownership of. Hence, many tax practitioners take the position that holding pre-cious metals/bullion in a bank safe deposit box in the name of the Self-Directed IRA LLC could satisfy the "physical possession" requirement under Internal

Revenue Code Section 408(m)(3)(B). However, the question, then becomes is the bank where the metals or coins are being stored in the name of the IRA LLC considered a trustee pursuant to IRC Section 408(a)?" John said.

"I was actually thinking about that same question." Mike said.

"The definition of a U.S. trustee is outlined in IRC Section 408(a), which discusses the definition of an IRA. So the argument goes if the IRS approved bullion/precious metals are held at a bank safe deposit box in the name of the LLC and the bank is not the trustee or the custodian of the IRA that hold the metals/bullion, then is the physical possession definition satisfied and is the bank acting as the trustee of the IRA which owns the metals. There are arguments on both sides. For example, IRC Section 408(m) also applies to 401(k) plans and the definition of a 401(k) plan trustee is not the same as a trustee of an IRA. Since the physical possession requirement outlined in IRC Section 408(m)(3)(B) applies to IRAs and 401(k) plans, some tax practitioners believe that the definition is satisfied so long as the bullion/metals are held at a bank or financial institution that satisfies the definition of trustee, as outlined in IRC Section 408(a), and not necessarily the actual trustee of the retirement account owning the bullion/metals. The language in IRC Section 408(m)(3)(B) uses the term "a" trustee" and not the "the" trustee" offering some support for the position that the coins can be held at any trustee, as defined under IRC 408(a) and not just the trustee of the IRA. This would make sense since a depository is considered a trustee pursuant to IRC Section 408(a), but may not be the actual trustee of the IRA owning the coins." John said.

"So what is your conclusion?" Mike asked.

I suggest that all my clients seeking to purchase IRS approved coins or precious metals/bullion with their retirement account hold them in the physical possession of a trustee, such as a depository. The IRS, as outlined in IRC 408(m)(3)(B) clearly does not allow any individual to hold IRS approved coins or precious metals/bullion personally, such as in their house. However, the Technical and Miscellaneous Revenue Act of 1988 Senate amendment seems to suggest that state minted coins can be held by a person other than the IRA holder, without referencing the term trustee, as defined in IRC Section 408. Nevertheless, we recommend that IRS approved coins should not be held personally by the IRA holder and should be held at a trustee, as defined in IRC 408.

For Self-Directed IRA LLC clients seeking to hold IRS approved coins and precious metals at a bank safe deposit box, we believe that this position has some risk, as the IRS has not offered any formal guidance. In the case of a Self-Directed IRA, if the bank where the safe deposit box is not the trustee of the IRA that purchased the metals or coins, an argument can be made that the metals or coins would not satisfy the physical possession definition outlined in IRC section 408 since the bank could not serve as the IRA trustee. This argument would seemingly not have much strength in the case of a Solo 401(k) plan, where an individual or individuals associated with the adopting employer would likely serve as the plan trustee and not the bank holding the plan's assets, thus not creating any trustee relationship between the bank and the plan, but still satisfying the definition of a trustee under IRC 408. In addition, the language in IRC Section 408(m)(3)(B) uses the term "a" trustee" and not the "the" trustee" offering some support for the position that the metals/bullion can be held at any trustee, as defined under IRC 408(a) and not just the trustee of the IRA holding the metals. This would make sense since a depository is considered a trustee pursuant to IRC 408(a), but may not be the actual trustee of the IRA that owns the coins or bullion/precious metals. Nevertheless, the safest approaching to holding IRS approved coins or bullion/precious metals is at a trustee, as defined in IRC Section 408, such as an approved depository. One thing that is clear, is the one should not ever hold IRS approved coins or precious metals/bullion personally.

In general, the rules surrounding the ownership and possession of IRS precious metals or coins are complicated. Therefore, it is crucial that one works with a tax attorney or tax professional that has the expertise and resources to help one safely navigate the IRS rules.

"Makes perfect sense," Mike said.

S CORPORATION INVESTMENTS

"In addition to the IRS–prohibited transaction rules outlined in the IRC Section 4975," John continued, "an IRA can't own stock in an S corporation."

"Why is that, again?" Mike asked.

"Because of the shareholder restrictions imposed on S corporations," John answered. "S corporations are C corporations that elect to pass corporate income, losses, deductions, and credits through to their shareholders for federal tax purposes. To qualify for S corporation status, the corporation must meet the following requirements:

- be a domestic corporation;
- have only allowable shareholders, including individuals, certain trusts, and estates;
- not include partnerships, corporations, or nonresident alien shareholders;
- have no more than one hundred shareholders; and
- have only one class of stock.

"Because an IRA is considered a trust for federal income-tax purposes," John continued, "and not treated as a permitted shareholder for an S corporation, having an IRA invest and become a shareholder would violate S corporation rules and cause the S election to be invalid, making the entity a C corporation again for tax purposes."

"But a retirement-account plan can own stock in a C corporation, right?" Mike asked.

"That's right."

"OK," Mike said, "I understand I can't engage in four categories of transactions with my retirement account:

(1) collectibles, with a special carve-out for precious metals and IRS-approved coins;
(2) life-insurance contracts with my IRA, but I may with my 401(k) plan, so long as the plan documents allow it;
(3) S corporation stock owned by an IRA; and
(4) any transaction that directly or indirectly personally benefits me or any other disqualified person—the IRC Section 4975 prohibited transactions."

"You got it," John said.

"I was just wondering something," Mike said. "Who determines whether I've engaged in a prohibited transaction?"

"That's actually a good question," John said. "Through an arrangement between the IRS and the Department of Labor (DOL), it's the DOL's responsibility to determine whether a specific transaction is a prohibited transaction and to issue prohibited-transaction exemptions. When the IRS discovers what appears to be a prohibited transaction in an individual's IRA, it turns the matter over to the DOL to make the determination. The DOL reviews the situation and responds to the IRS, which in turn responds to the taxpayer. If the IRA grantor wants to apply for a prohibited-transaction exemption, he or she must apply to the DOL."

"So does the DOL issue the exemptions?" Mike asked.

"It does have that authority," John said. "What's known as 'prohibitive transaction class exemptions,' or PTCEs, are available for anyone, while another class of exemptions, called individual prohibited-transaction exemptions, or PTEs, are issued only to the applicant."

PENALTIES FOR ENGAGING IN A PROHIBITED TRANSACTION

"This makes sense to me," Mike said, "but I was wondering, what are the IRS penalties if someone does engage in an IRS-prohibited transaction?"

"As you can imagine," John said, "the penalties are quite steep. The IRS needs to make them painful in order to protect the distribution-taxation rules, which are a big revenue source for the government."

"I get it," Mike said.

"In general," John continued, "the penalty under IRC Section 4975 generally starts out at 15 percent for most types of retirement plans."

"Wow," Mike said, "that is harsh."

"Actually," John said, "it's even harsher for IRAs. In general, if the IRA holder (IRA owner) or IRA beneficiary engages in a transaction that violates the prohibited-transaction rules set forth under IRC Section 4975, the individual's IRA would lose its tax-exempt status and the entire fair market value of the IRA would be treated as a taxable distribution, subject to ordinary income tax. In addition, the IRA holder or beneficiary would be subject to a minimum penalty of 15 percent as well as a 10 percent early-distribution penalty if the IRA holder or beneficiary is under the age of 59½."

"Holy cow," Mike said.

"Yeah," John said. "Although the penalty for engaging in a prohibited transaction generally starts out at 15 percent for most types of retirement plans, the penalty is more severe for IRAs. The initial tax on a prohibited transaction is 15 percent of the amount involved for each year (or part of a year) in the taxable period. If the transaction is not corrected within the taxable period, an additional tax of 100 percent of the amount involved is imposed. Both taxes are payable by any disqualified person who participated in the transaction (other than a fiduciary acting only as such). If more than one person takes part in the transaction, each person can be jointly and severally liable for the entire tax. According to Code Section 408(e), when an IRA is involved in a transaction that is prohibited under IRC Section 4975, the IRA loses its tax-exempt status, and the IRA holder is treated as receiving a distribution on the first day of the tax year in which the prohibited transaction occurred. The distribution amount that the IRA holder is deemed to have received is equal to the fair market value of the IRA as of the first day of such tax year. In other words, the entire IRA is blown up and no longer treated as an IRA as of the first day of the taxable year in which the prohibited transaction occurred."

"I want to avoid that," Mike said.

"The good thing when it comes to prohibited-transaction penalties," John said, "is that they are easily avoidable."

"Are the penalties for a prohibited transaction the same for an IRA and a 401(k) plan?" Mike asked.

"Great question. Actually, the penalty for engaging in a prohibited transaction is harsher for an IRA than a 401(k) plan. When an IRA holder or beneficiary is involved in a prohibited transaction pursuant to IRC Section 4975, the IRA loses its tax-exempt status on the first day of the tax year in which the prohibited transaction occurred. Whereas, in the case of a 401(k) plan, the entire plan would not lose its tax exempt status, only the prohibited transaction would be penalized," John explained.

"Basically," Mike said, "just don't engage in a prohibited transaction, and you have nothing to worry about."

"Exactly," John said. "For most retirement investors who will be investing in stocks and other traditional financial products, there is really not much to worry about when it comes to a prohibited transaction. The likelihood of engaging in a prohibited transaction in such circumstance is almost impossible, especially if you are buying stocks, mutual funds, and ETFS from a major financial institution. But, for a retirement-account investor looking to make nontraditional investments, such as real estate, private loans, and precious metals, you really need to make yourself aware of the prohibited-transaction rules because of the harsh penalties."

"I get it," Mike said. "Investor beware."

"The prohibited-transaction rules are extremely broad," John noted. "So a retirement-account investor looking to engage in certain nontraditional investments must be especially cautious and should consult a tax attorney or CPA with specific questions."

"I promise," Mike said.

"It's critical to understand what you can't do when it comes to the IRS," John said. "We need this information in advance before making important decisions about how we will invest or allocate our retirement-account assets. But I think it's time we start talking about the type of investments you can make with a self-directed IRA," John said.

"That sounds great. Same time tomorrow?" Mike said.

"Perfect," John responded.

5

USING A SELF-DIRECTED IRA
TO MAKE INVESTMENTS

M IKE GAVE JOHN a call at the set time.

"All right," John said. "We've now spent a lot of time discussing the different types of self-directed IRA accounts, as well as the prohibited transaction rules. So now I think it's a good time to focus on how to make investments with a self-directed IRA, what types of investments can be made, and which investments are popular. Once we review the types of investments that are typically made with a self-directed IRA, the IRS prohibited transactions rules we discussed will make a lot more sense.

"OK," Mike said. "That makes sense. Jen and I are particularly interested in real estate, so I hope we'll cover how to make real estate investments with a self-directed IRA."

"Absolutely," John agreed. "In addition, we'll also talk about some of the other popular self-directed IRA investments, such as precious metals, hard-money lending, tax liens, and private business investments."

"Whenever I talk about retirement funds with friends now, they are all convinced that their retirement funds must be invested in bank CDs, the stock market, or mutual funds. Amazing, isn't it?"

"As I've mentioned a few times now," John said, "traditional financial institutions have no incentive to publicize the advantages of self-directed IRA accounts or inform people that IRA account holders have the ability to make nontraditional investments with their retirement funds. In fact, the IRS does give retirement account holders the ability to make all sorts of traditional as well as nontraditional investments using IRA funds; you just need to make sure your plan documents allow for it. The IRS can't force any of the major financial institutions to allow you to buy gold, real estate, or make private loans, but you do have options to go elsewhere."

"I love that aspect," Mike said.

"That's the main advantage of the self-directed IRA," John agreed. "You gain tremendous latitude and freedom to invest your plan assets and grow them in the way that suits your needs, interests, and personal expertise."

"So what kind of investments can you make?" Mike asked.

"Check your e-mail inbox. I just sent you an e-mail with a number of attachments," John said.

Mike opened the e-mail and clicked on the first attachment. The document outlined the most popular types of investments available for retirement accounts. "Remember, as long as your IRA custodian allows it, or—in the case of a checkbook control IRA LLC—the investment does not violate IRS prohibited transaction rules under IRC Section 4975, or is not a collectible or life insurance contract pursuant to IRC Section 408(m), you can enjoy the benefits of tax-deferred or (in the case of a self-directed Roth IRA) tax-free income and gains."

- Residential or commercial real estate
- Raw land
- Foreclosure property
- Mortgages
- Mortgage pools
- Deeds
- Private loans
- Tax liens
- Private businesses
- Limited Liability Companies

- Limited Liability Partnerships
- Private placements
- Precious metals and certain coins
- Stocks, bonds, mutual funds
- Foreign currencies

"That's quite a range of options," Mike said.

"It is," John agreed. "So let's look more closely at the main groups. I want to paint you a clear picture of what you can do, and provide you with some helpful tips for making investments that can enable you to achieve your investment goals."

"Thanks," Mike said.

"Let's start with using a self-directed IRA to purchase real estate."

REAL ESTATE

"Real estate has become one of the most popular nontraditional-investment options for IRA and Roth IRA investors. According to a McKinsey & Company report, "The Mainstreaming of Alternative Investments: Fueling the Next Wave of Growth in Asset Management," by Onur Erzan, principal, dated June 2012, in the United States, institutional investors expect to have 28 percent of their portfolios allocated to alternative investments by the end of 2013, up from 26 percent in 2010. That quote was taken from a recent *Financial Advisor* magazine article. The same piece also referenced a multiyear McKinsey & Company study that noted year-end 2011 assets under management for global alternatives reached record levels of $6.5 trillion, having grown at a five-year rate of over seven times that of traditional asset classes," John said.

"Real estate offers diversification from overexposure to Wall Street for both personal and retirement funds. After the 2008 financial crisis, many retirement investors began to appreciate the importance of having a well-balanced and diversified retirement portfolio that can help protect against another financial crisis. People generally like to invest in something they know and understand. Real estate is reemerging as an asset class that more Americans have confidence and comfort in compared to the vagaries of the stock market. Buying tangible assets, such as real estate, is seen as a solid way of protecting retirement savings from the threat of inflation," John added.

"Plus, all income and gains from real estate owned in a self-directed IRA are exempt from tax, making real estate an even more powerful investment. For example, if you purchased a piece of property with your self-directed IRA for $100,000 and you later sold the property for $300,000, the $200,000 of gain appreciation would generally be tax-free. Whereas, if you purchased the property using personal funds (nonretirement funds), the gain would be subject to federal income tax and, in most cases, state income tax," John said.

"The IRS allows you to use a self-directed Roth IRA to purchase real estate or raw land, as long as your plan allows for it. Remember, it is up to the IRA custodian whether nontraditional-investment options, such as real estate, are permitted to be made with IRA or Roth IRA funds. In general, most financial institution–established IRAs do not allow for real estate investments, while a custodian-directed and checkbook control self-directed IRA will allow for the real estate investment option. If you elect to use a checkbook control self-directed Roth IRA LLC, as manager of the self-directed IRA LLC, making a real estate investment is as simple as writing a check from your self-directed IRA LLC bank account," John stated.

TAX LIENS AND TAX DEEDS

"Tax-lien and tax-deed investments have become popular investment choices for many self-directed IRA investors. Beginning in 2009, as foreclosures continued to pile up, many properties were saddled with unpaid property taxes. For some investors, this created a great investment opportunity," John noted.

"Tax collectors in twenty-nine states as well as Washington, DC; Puerto Rico; and the US Virgin Islands use tax-lien sales to force owners to pay unpaid property taxes. The process varies by state, but here's how it generally works: When property owners don't pony up for their property taxes, tax collectors wait out the time period required by state law and then put those unpaid property taxes up for auction. The time period varies from just a few months to several years depending on the state. In most states, the person willing to pay the most cash for the tax lien wins the auction. Some states, however, have a bid-down process, in which investors' bids indicate how much interest they're willing to accept on their investment, and the lowest bidder wins. Whatever method is used, the tax collector takes the payment for the overdue taxes from the winning bidder. In exchange, the purchaser gets a lien on the property. As the winning bidder, you'd get a return on your investment in one of two ways: interest on your bid amount or ownership of the property," John added.

"With a tax deed, on the other hand, you will actually own the property in which the owner has been delinquent in paying the property taxes. A tax-deed sale generally involves property being sold by a taxing authority or the court to recover delinquent taxes. The IRS permits the purchase of tax liens and tax deeds with a self-directed IRA. The advantage of purchasing tax liens or tax deeds with a self-directed IRA is that your profits are tax-deferred back into your retirement account until a distribution is taken. In the case of a self-directed Roth IRA, all gains are tax-free," John stated.

"For tax liens and tax deeds, I believe the checkbook IRA is a far more viable option than the custodian-controlled self-directed IRA, as the purchase of tax liens and tax deeds requires immediate payment of funds, typically at auction, which is close to impossible with a custodian-controlled self-directed IRA," John said.

LOANS AND NOTES

"The IRS permits using IRA or Roth IRA funds to make loans or purchase notes from third parties. By using a self-directed IRA to make loans or purchase notes from third parties, all interest payments received are tax deferred until a distribution is taken. In the case of a self-directed Roth IRA, all gains are tax free. When engaging in private lending transactions or purchasing notes, it is important to make note of the IRS–prohibited transaction and disqualified-person rules, which are found in IRC Section 4975. For example, if you used a self-directed Roth IRA to loan money to a friend, all interest received would flow back into your self-directed IRA, whereas if you lent your friend money from personal funds (nonretirement funds), the interest received would be subject to federal and, in most cases, state income tax," John illuminated.

PRECIOUS METALS AND COINS
"You can also use your self-directed assets to make investments in precious metals and certain coins. The advantage of using a self-directed Roth IRA to purchase precious metals and/or coins is that there is an argument that values generally keep up with, or exceed, inflation rates better than other investments. The IRS under IRC Section 408(m) provides a detailed overview of the types of metals and coins that can be purchased with retirement funds. We will discuss the types of IRS-approved precious metals when we discuss the prohibited-transaction rules," John mentioned.

FOREIGN CURRENCIES AND OPTIONS
"There is no IRS prohibition against using retirement funds to purchase foreign currencies or engage in option trading. Many investors believe that foreign-currency investments offer liquidity advantages compared to the stock market as well as significant investment opportunities. With respect to option trading, there is a belief that it can potentially generate increased cost efficiency, may be less risky than equities, and has the potential to deliver higher-percentage returns. Again, all foreign-currency gains and income from the lapse or termination of an option are generally tax deferred until a distribution is taken, and in the case of a self-directed Roth IRA, all gains are tax free," John said.

STOCKS, BONDS, MUTUAL FUNDS, CDs
"In addition to nontraditional investments such as real estate, a self-directed IRA or Roth IRA may also purchase stocks, bonds, mutual funds, and CDs.

According to the Investment Company Institute report, "The IRA Investor Profile: The Traditional IRA Investors' Activity, 2007–2012," dated March 10, 2014, traditional IRA investors' allocation to equity holdings fell, on average, although some of the change merely reflects market movement rather than investors' rebalancing. For example, among consistent traditional IRA investors aged twenty-five to fifty-nine, about three-quarters of their traditional IRA assets were invested in equity holdings—which includes equities, equity funds, and the equity portion of balanced funds—at year-end 2007, and about two-thirds of their traditional IRA assets were invested in equity holdings at year-end 2012. Accordingly, it's easy to conclude that stocks, mutual funds, ETFs, and other equities are by far the most popular investment for retirement accounts," John said.

"The advantage of using a self-directed IRA or Roth IRA with checkbook control is that you are not limited to just making these types of investments. You can open a stock-trading account with any financial institution. No one is arguing against stocks as the best retirement investment. Indeed, history has shown that owning stocks is one of the easiest and most profitable ways to grow your wealth over the long term. From January 1, 1900, through December 31, 2013, for example, the average return of the S&P 500, which tracks the 500 largest stocks based on market capitalization, was 11.6 percent. Stocks have proven to be a good investment over time. Could you do better with a different investment? Possibly. The bigger concern, however, is that such heavy exposure to the US equity markets carries some risk. Diversification is a must when it comes to retirement planning," John added.

USING A SELF-DIRECTED IRA TO INVEST IN A BUSINESS

"Curious, can I use my IRA to invest in my business and shelter all income from tax?" Mike asked.

"Unfortunately, no," John said. "The same prohibited-transaction rules that apply to traditional IRAs also apply to Roth IRAs. We will go into all the IRS–prohibited transaction rules in detail in the future, so don't worry. So, just as you are not permitted to invest your traditional IRA in your own business, as it would violate the prohibited-transaction rules under IRC Section 4975, the same rules would apply to Roth IRAs. Imagine if you can invest your Roth IRA funds in your own business and shelter all the income tax for your business. That would be pretty nice but, unfortunately, the IRS doesn't feel the same way. In fact, the IRS has issued a number of letter rulings outlining this exact type of situation, so it is highly risky to try to use a Roth IRA to shelter personal or business income. Not only could it trigger civil penalties, but the IRS could also pursue criminal charges," John noted.

"What about investing an IRA in a friend's business? Can I shelter all income from tax?"

"Yes and no," John said. "On the yes side, just like with a traditional IRA, you could use a self-directed Roth IRA to invest in a friend's business or any nondisqualified person's business. However, if the business is being conducted via an LLC or other flow-through entity, a set of tax rules known as the Unrelated Business Taxable Income (UBTI or UBIT) would kick in and could potentially impose close to a 40 percent tax on the business income allocated to your Roth IRA. So, it would turn your potentially tax-free investment into a very tax-unfriendly investment. You would need to run the numbers and see how the UBTI or UBIT tax would affect your expected returns, and you would need to determine whether using personal funds instead of Roth IRA funds would make more sense."

"What exactly is UBTI?" Mike asked.

UBTI

"Let me explain," explained John. "In general, if you make passive investments with your self-directed IRA, such as stocks, mutual funds, precious metals, foreign currency, and rental real estate, the income generated by the investment will not be subject to any tax. Only if your self-directed IRA makes investments into an active business, such as a retail store, restaurant, real estate–development business, or software company, using a pass-through entity such as an LLC or partnership, will your self-directed IRA likely be subject to a tax known as the unrelated business taxable income tax, also known as UBTI or UBIT."

"Can you give me another example?" Mike asked.

"Let's say a self-directed IRA invests in an LLC that operates an active business such as a restaurant or water franchise; the income or gains generated from the investment will generally be subject to the UBTI tax. However, if the self-directed IRA invested in an active business through a C corporation, such as Apple or Google, there would be no UBTI since the C Corporation acts as a blocker blocking the income from flowing through to the self-directed IRA shareholder. A C Corporation is an entity taxed separately from its shareholders (blocker corporation), whereas an LLC is treated as a partnership or pass-through entity (flow-through) for tax purposes. This is why most Americans have never heard of the UBTI rules and why you can invest your IRA into a public company. Since almost all public companies traded on the public markets or that make up mutual funds, such as Apple, Google, J.P. Morgan, or GE, are C Corporations, they block the application of the UBTI tax since the income from the C Corporation gets trapped at the corporate level and does not flow through to the shareholders. Remember that if an IRA makes a passive investment, such as rental income, dividends, and royalties, such income will not be subject to the UBTI rules pursuant to IRC Section 512."

"I'm still not sure I get it," Mike laughed.

"Here we go," John said. "One of the advantages of using retirement funds through your self-directed IRA to make investments is that, in most cases, all income and gains from the investments flow back to your IRA LLC tax-free. This is because an IRA is exempt from tax, pursuant to IRC Section 408. Pursuant to IRC Section 512, most of the popular forms of income generated by a retirement income will be exempt from tax. This is why most American investors look at you funny when you start telling them about the Unrelated Business Taxable Income rules, also known as UBTI or UBIT, which trigger a tax on certain categories of retirement-account income."

"I know; I never hear about it," Mike said. "OK, makes sense."

"The good thing about the UBTI rules is that they won't apply to over 90 percent of American retirement investors because most types of income and gains generated by a retirement account are exempt from the UBTI rules. The IRC exempts dividends, interest, capital gains, royalties, and rental income from being subject to the UBTI tax rules. Even so, the UBTI rules are new and somewhat intimidating to most people when learning about them for the first time. For example, buying public stocks and mutual funds with a self-directed IRA will not trigger the UBTI; neither would receiving a dividend from a public stock or interest from a bond or even rental income from an investment property. In the case of a self-directed IRA, the UBTI tax is essentially triggered in three main types of investments:

1. Investing in an active trade or business via a pass-through entity, such as an LLC
2. Using margin when buying stock
3. Using a nonrecourse loan to buy real estate

"Before I go through the three ways the UBTI tax can be triggered when using a self-directed IRA, I think it is helpful to examine why the UBTI tax came into law," John stated.

"What's the backstory on that?" Mike asked.

"It's pretty interesting," John enthused. "Back in the 1950s, Congress was concerned that for-profit companies would set up a charity and run their business through a charity and escape taxation forever, thus, providing them with an unfair advantage because of their tax-exempt status. With that in mind, they created the UBTI rules under IRC Section 512. These rules can be found under IRC Sections 511–514 and have become known as the Unrelated Business Taxable Income rules, also known as UBTI or UBIT. If the UBTI rules are triggered, the income generated from those activities will generally be subjected to a tax of approximately 35 percent. Of note, a self-directed IRA investing in an active trade or business using a C Corporation, which consists of almost all public-stock companies and mutual funds, will not trigger the UBTI tax. The reason is that a C Corporation is not a pass-through entity, and so the C Corporation essentially 'blocks' the income from traveling to the shareholders, thus blocking the active trade or business income from flowing to the IRA. You can think of a C Corporation as a box and an LLC or partnership as a funnel, which I think helps to understand why the UBTI tax would not apply to a retirement account owning shares in a C Corporation."

"What is Unrelated Business Taxable Income?" Mike asked.

"UBTI is defined as 'gross income derived by any organization from any unrelated trade or business regularly carried on by it, reduced by deductions directly connected with the business.' The UBTI rules only apply to exempt organizations such as charities, IRAs, and 401(k) plans. With the enactment of ERISA in 1974, IRAs and 401(k) plans, which are considered tax-exempt parties pursuant to IRC Sections 408 and 401, respectively, became subject to the UBTI rules. As a result, if an IRA or 401(k) plan invests in an active business through an LLC or partnership, the income generated by the IRA or 401(k) from the active business investment will be subject to the UBTI rules."

"OK," Mike said.

"In the case of a self-directed IRA or Roth IRA, a transaction would not trigger the UBTI or UBIT rules if the transaction is not considered a trade or business that is regularly carried on. This typically involves passive types of activities that generate capital gains, interest, rental income, royalties, and dividends, the categories of income exempt according to IRC Section 512, which are also the most popular investments for retirement accounts. However, if the tax-exempt organization (your retirement account) engages in an active trade or business that is regularly carried on, such as a restaurant, store, or manufacturing business, the IRS will tax the income."

"What's the UBTI tax rate?" Mike asked.

"IRC 511 taxes 'unrelated business taxable income' at the rates applicable to corporations or trusts, depending on the organization's legal characteristics. In general, a self-directed IRA subject to UBTI is taxed at the trust-tax rate because an IRA is considered a trust. For 2016, a retirement account subject to UBTI can be subject to a tax of close to 40 percent."

Mike looked up. "Pretty steep."

"Yes. In fact, they're higher than most individuals' income-tax rates as well as the corporation income-tax rate. This is one of the main reasons why the UBTI tax rules are so important to understand and avoid if possible. In essence, the UBTI tax is imposed on the retirement-account investment and actually creates a double-tax regime, since the UBTI tax will apply in the year the income or gain is realized and then also when the plan participant takes a distribution or is required to take a distribution after the age of 70½ (in the case of a pretax IRA). This is just another reason why it is important to be aware of the UBTI tax rules and their potential application to retirement-account investments.

"So, the question is what level of business activity must you cross before triggering the UBTI or UBIT tax? Unfortunately, there is no clear test as to how much business activity one must engage in in a given year in order to trigger the UBTI or UBIT tax. In general, the IRS has a number of factors it will examine to determine whether one has engaged in a high enough volume of transactions to trigger the UBTI tax. First, the IRS will examine the frequency of the transactions: How many business transactions are done in a year? Second, the IRS will examine the intent of the person: Was the person intending to engage in an active trade or business? Third, the IRS will look at the scope of other activities of the retirement account to determine whether the activity is part of a business activity or an investment. Fourth, the IRS will look at the personal business activities of the IRA investor to help determine whether the IRA investment is part of an overall business model. So, for example, several real estate flips by Donald Trump's self-directed IRA could look more like a business than if they were made by a teacher or accountant."

"I am sorry I am asking so many questions," Mike said, "but if I ended up using a self-directed Roth IRA to buy real estate, I could see myself doing multiple small real estate deals in a year, and I need to know that the transactions would not trigger the UBTI tax rules. So just to be clear, the determination of whether an activity is an active trade or business and will, thus, trigger the UBTI or UBIT tax, which is taxed at a rate of approximately 35 percent, depends on the facts and circumstances."

"Yes," John agreed. "Clearly, if you have a store, restaurant, or manufacturing plant, you are undoubtedly in business. But for some startups or real estate transactions, there can be a question as to whether the activity is a simple investment or hobby or whether the activity rises to the level of a trade or business. Thankfully, the IRS has issued some guidance as to whether an activity is a hobby or investment."

John opened the Internet browser on his smartphone and pulled up the IRS page. He started reading to Mike:

"In order to make this determination of whether an activity is a business or hobby, taxpayers should consider the following factors:

- Does the time and effort put into the activity indicate an intention to make a profit?
- Does the taxpayer depend on income from the activity?
- If there are losses, are they due to circumstances beyond the taxpayer's control, or did they occur in the startup phase of the business?
- Has the taxpayer changed methods of operation to improve profitability?
- Does the taxpayer or his or her advisers have the knowledge needed to carry on the activity as a successful business?
- Has the taxpayer made a profit in similar activities in the past?
- Does the activity make a profit in some years?
- Can the taxpayer expect to make a profit in the future from the appreciation of assets used in the activity?

"OK, this is really helpful," Mike said. "I can see how doing multiple real estate transactions can potentially be an issue."

"Yes, you are 100 percent right; the determination of whether a set of real estate activities is treated as an investment or a business and, thus, subject to the UBTI taxing regime, can be somewhat tricky. Pretty important stuff, considering that retirement accounts don't pay tax on investments but investing in an active business through a pass-through entity would be subject to the UBTI tax," stated John.

"OK, I think I am starting to understand the UBTI rules and their potential impact on retirement-account investments. As long as a retirement account did not use margin, a nonrecourse loan, or invest in an active trade or business through a pass-through entity, such as an LLC, the UBTI rules would not apply," Mike said.

"Exactly," John said.

"One last question: Can I take a loan from a self-directed IRA or Roth IRA?" Mike asked.

"Unfortunately not," John said. "You cannot borrow any funds from an IRA without triggering an IRS-prohibited transaction. However, if you are a participant in an employer 401(k) plan or are self-employed and can adopt a Solo 401(k) plan, you are able to borrow the lesser of $50,000 or 50 percent of your 401(k) plan account value and use the loan for any purpose."

"OK, that sounds great. What about something called a ROBS? I know one of my friends' wives who used that structure recently to purchase a franchise. I am sorry if it is a bit off topic, but do you mind explaining to me how it works?" Mike asked.

"I am happy you brought the ROBS structure up because it is something I did want to chat about at some point. When it comes to using retirement funds to buy or finance a business that you or another disqualified person will be involved in personally, there is only one legal way to do it and that is through the business acquisition solution, also known as a rollover business start-up solution (ROBS). The ROBS solution takes advantage of an exception in the Tax Code under IRC Section 4975(d) that allows one to use 401(k) plan funds to buy stock in a C corporation, which is known as qualifying employer securities. The exception to the IRS–prohibited transaction rules found in IRC Section 4975(d)(13) requires that a 401(k) plan buy qualifying employer securities, which is defined as stock of a C corporation. This is the reason one cannot use a self-directed IRA LLC to invest in a business the IRA holder or a disqualified person will be personally involved in, or why a 401(k) plan cannot invest in an LLC in which the plan participant or disqualified person will be involved, without triggering the prohibited-transaction rules. Hence, in order to use retirement funds to invest in a business in which a disqualified person will be personally involved, one needs a C corporation to operate a business and adopt a 401(k) plan."

"How does the ROBS arrangement work?" Mike asked.

"The ROBS arrangement typically involves rolling over a prior IRA or 401(k) plan account into a newly established 401(k) plan, which either an already existing or a newly established C corporation business sponsored, and then investing the rollover 401(k) plan funds in the stock of the C corporation. The funds are then deposited in the C corporation bank account and are available for use for business purposes."

"So what is the difference between using a self-directed IRA versus the ROBS structure to buy a business?" Mike asked.

"In a lot of respects, using a self-directed IRA LLC or a 401(k) plan to purchase stock in a corporation would seem to be subject to the same rules. However, as described above, using 401(k) plan funds and not IRA funds allows one to take advantage of the prohibited-transaction exemption under IRC Section 4975(d)(13) for qualifying employer securities. In essence, if one uses an IRA to buy an interest in a new business he or she was personally involved in, that transaction would likely violate the IRS–prohibited transaction rules and would not satisfy the exception in the Tax Code under IRC Section 4975(d). This is because the exception would only apply if a 401(k) plan and C corporation are used and the 401(k) plan purchased stock in the adopting employer C corporation stock."

"That's helpful," Mike said.

"The limitation of using a self-directed IRA LLC to buy a business is that the individual retirement-account business owner would not be able to be actively involved in the business, earn a salary, or even personally guarantee a business loan; whereas, if the business owner uses a ROBS strategy, that individual would be able to be actively involved in the business and earn a salary without triggering the IRS–prohibited transaction rules."

"Any downside to using the ROBS?" Mike asked.

"Yes—a few. Without going into much detail, as it is a bit off topic since you and Jen are not considering using retirement funds to buy a business, I would say that the requirement to use a C Corporation, which isn't the most tax-efficient business entity due to its two levels of taxation, is the major downside. The others are fees and IRS-compliance issues involving valuing the business assets being purchased as well as administering the 401(k) plan, John explained.

"One more thing. How is the self-directed IRA when it comes to asset and creditor protection?" Mike asked.

"Great question. Thanks for reminding me—I wanted to touch on this before we finished for the day. Retirement accounts have become many Americans' most valuable assets. That means it is vital that you have the ability to protect them from creditors, such as people who have won lawsuits against you. In general, the asset/creditor protection strategies available to you depend on the type of retirement account you have (i.e., traditional IRA, Roth IRA, or 401(k) qualified retirement plan), your state residency, and whether the assets are yours or have been inherited. When it comes to IRA asset protection in the case of personal bankruptcy of the IRA holder, like 401(k) qualified plans, the Bankruptcy Abuse Prevention and Consumer Protection Act of 2005 ("BAPCPA" or the "Act"), effective for bankruptcies filed after October 17, 2005, provides protection to a debtor's IRA funds by way of exempting them from the bankruptcy estate. The general exemption found in section 522 of the Bankruptcy Code, 11 U.S.C. §522, provides an unlimited exemption for IRAs under Section 408 and Roth IRAs under Section 408A. The exemption for IRAs is limited to $1,000,000.The $1,000,000 has been increased by a cost of living adjustment to $1,171,650. However, the $1,000,000 limit does not apply to employer-sponsored IRAs (e.g., SEPs or SIMPLEs). Additionally, rollovers into IRAs from qualified plans are not subject to the $1,000,000 limit. In other words, SEPs, SIMPLEs, and IRA rollovers from qualified plans have an unlimited exemption. It appears that a rollover from a SEP or SIMPLE IRA receives only $1,000,000 of protection. John noted.

"Interesting. What about asset and creditor protection for my IRA outside of bankruptcy?" Mike asked.

"In general, ERISA pension plans, such as 401(k) qualified plans, are afforded extensive anti-alienation creditor protection both inside and outside of bankruptcy. However, these extensive anti-alienation protections do not extend to an IRA, including a self-directed IRA arrangement under code Section 408. Therefore, since an individually established and funded traditional or

Roth IRA is not an ERISA pension plan, IRAs are not preempted under ERISA. Thus, for anything short of bankruptcy, state law determines whether IRAs (including Roth IRAs) are shielded from creditors' claims," John said.

"OK. What is the consensus among the states, if any, on this subject?" Mike asked.

"Most states actually offer IRAs full protection from creditors outside of bankruptcy, but some states, like California and Wyoming, do not offer full exemption, while others, such as Alabama, limit the exemption protection to non-Roth IRAs. In any case, I would suggest discussing your particular situation with a local attorney or CPA," John recommended.

"Gotcha. Next week, same time and place?" Mike asked.

"Yes. Let's finish up by going through a few case studies of how one can make a self-directed IRA investment using a custodian-controlled or checkbook control self-directed IRA," John said.

"Sounds great," Mike responded.

6

A STEP-BY-STEP OVERVIEW OF HOW TO MAKE A SELF-DIRECTED IRA INVESTMENT

B ECAUSE JOHN WAS going to go through a step-by-step outline of how to set up and use a self-directed IRA to make real estate and other IRS-approved investments, Mike wanted Jen to be on the call. Mike and Jen called John at the scheduled time. After some small talk, John got right into it.

"I think it would be smart, for Jen's purposes, to just do a quick review of what a self-directed IRA is. Most people mistakenly believe that their IRA must be invested in bank CDs, the stock market, or mutual funds. Few investors realize that the IRS has always permitted real estate to be held inside IRA retirement accounts. Investments in real estate with a self-directed IRA are fully permissible under the Employee Retirement Income Security Act of 1974 (ERISA). IRS rules permit you to engage in almost any type of real estate investment, aside generally from any investment involving a disqualified person," John said.

"In addition, the IRS states the following on its website: 'IRA law does not prohibit investing in real estate but Trustees are not required to offer real estate as an option.'"

John added: "Income or gains generated by an IRA generate tax-deferred/tax-free profits. Using a self-directed IRA to purchase real estate allows the IRA to earn tax-free income/gains and pay taxes at a future date (in the case of a Roth IRA, the income/gains are always tax-free), rather than within the year the investment produces income. With a self-directed IRA, you can invest tax-free and not have to pay taxes right away—or in the case of a Roth IRA—ever! All the income or gains from your real estate deals flow through to your IRA tax-free," John stated.

"There are essentially three types of self-directed IRA accounts," John continued: "(i) a financial institution self-directed IRA, which essentially allows you to select between a number of traditional equity investments, such as stock, mutual funds, and ETFs, (ii) a custodian-controlled self-directed IRA, which involves a trust company or IRA custodian, which allows you to make traditional as well as alternative asset investments, such as in real estate, using your IRA, and (iii) a checkbook control self-directed IRA, which involves the establishment of an LLC wholly owned by the IRA and managed by the IRA holder, allowing the manager of the LLC to make investments simply by writing a check.".

"OK—thanks. That is really helpful," Jen said.

"Good—establishing and funding a custodian-controlled or checkbook control self-directed IRA pretty much works the same way, except for the part involving the LLC," John added.

"The first step to making an investment, such as in real estate, with a self-directed IRA is establishing an IRA account with an IRA custodian, such as the IRA Financial Trust Company. In general, the first question you will need to ask yourself is what type of retirement funds you wish to use in your self-directed IRA. It is generally possible to rollover or transfer any type of retirement funds to a self-directed IRA LLC, including:

- Traditional IRA
- Roth IRA
- SEP
- SIMPLE
- 401(k)
- 403(b)
- Plans for Self-Employed (Keoghs)

- ESOPs
- Money Purchase Pensions Plans

"All this information will be important in terms of helping you complete the self-directed IRA account application and open the right self-directed IRA account," John said.

"How do I fund a self-directed IRA? Jen asked.

"In general, a self-directed IRA LLC may be funded by a transfer from another IRA account or through a rollover from an eligible defined contribution plan. Eligible defined contribution plans include qualified 401(k) retirement plans under IRC Sections 401(a), 403(a), 403(b), and governmental 457(b) plans. Transfers and rollovers are types of transactions that allow movements of assets between like IRAs—traditional IRA to traditional IRA and Roth IRA to Roth IRA. An IRA transfer is the most common method of funding a self-directed IRA LLC or self-directed Roth IRA," John stated.

IRA TRANSFERS TO A SELF-DIRECTED IRA WITH A TRADITIONAL IRA

"An IRA-to-IRA transfer is one of the most common methods of moving assets from one IRA to another. A transfer usually occurs between two separate financial organizations, but a transfer may also occur between IRAs held at the same organization. If an IRA transfer is handled correctly, the transfer is not taxable. With an IRA transfer, the IRA holder directs the transfer, but does not actually receive the IRA assets. Instead, the transaction is completed by the distributing and receiving financial institutions. In order for the IRA transfer to be tax-free and penalty-free, the IRA holder must not receive the IRA funds in a transfer. Rather, the check must be made payable to the new IRA custodian. Also, there is no reporting or withholding to the IRS on an IRA transfer. The self-directed IRA custodian specialists can assist you in funding your self-directed IRA LLC by transferring your current pretax or after-tax IRA funds to your new self-directed IRA or self-directed Roth IRA structure tax-free and penalty-free," John stated.

"The way the transfer works," John continued, "is that the new custodian, with your consent, will request the transfer of IRA assets from your existing IRA custodian in a tax-free and penalty-free IRA transfer. Once the IRA funds are either transferred by wire or check tax-free to the new IRA custodian, the new custodian will be able to invest the IRA assets at your direction, either to make the investment or into the LLC, where you will gain checkbook control."

"What about moving funds from a 401(k) plan to a self-directed IRA?" Jen asked.

"Since 2002," John responded, "individuals may rollover both pretax and after-tax 401(k) plan fund assets from 401(a), 403(a), 403(b), and governmental 457(b) plans into a traditional IRA tax-free and penalty-free. In general, in order to rollover qualified retirement plans to a traditional IRA there must be a plan-triggering event. A plan-triggering event is typically based on the plan documents, but they generally include the following: (i) the termination of the plan, (ii) the plan participant reaching the age of 59½, or (iii) the plan participant leaving the employer," John stated.

"I have heard of a direct rollover—what is the difference between a direct and an indirect rollover? Jen asked.

"Super question. A direct rollover occurs when a plan participant, who has access to his or her retirement funds, moves the eligible qualified retirement plan funds to an IRA custodian. In other words, a direct rollover is between a qualified retirement plan and an IRA, whereas a transfer is between IRA financial institutions.

How to Complete a Direct Rollover

A retirement tax professional will work with you to establish a new self-directed IRA account at a new IRA custodian. With a direct rollover from a defined contribution plan (i.e., 401(k) plan), the plan participant must initiate the direct rollover request. This means the plan participant and not the IRA custodian must request the movement of 401(k) plan funds to the new IRA custodian. A retirement tax professional will assist you in completing the direct rollover request form, which will allow you to move your 401(k), 403(a), 403(b), 457(b), or defined benefit plan assets to your new IRA account.

A direct rollover may be accomplished by any reasonable means of direct payment to an IRA. Regulations state that the reasonable means may include wire transfer, mailing a check to the new IRA custodian, or mailing a check, made out to the new IRA custodian, to the plan participant.

ROLLOVER CHART

John sent Mike and Jen an e-mail, including an attachment of an IRS chart, that summarized all the IRA rollover rules.

Exhibit E

ROLLOVER CHART

6/7/2011

Roll From \ Roll To	Roth IRA	IRA (traditional)	SIMPLE IRA	SEP-IRA	457(b) (government)	Qualified Plan [1] (pre-tax)	403(b) (pre-tax)	Designated Roth Account (401(k), 403(b) or 457(b)[2])
Roth IRA	YES	NO	NO	NO	NO	NO	NO	NO
IRA (traditional)	YES[3]	YES	NO	YES	YES[4]	YES	YES	NO
SIMPLE IRA	YES,[3] after two years	YES, after two years	YES	YES, after two years	YES,[4] after two years	YES, after two years	YES, after two years	NO
SEP-IRA	YES[3]	YES	NO	YES	YES[4]	YES	YES	NO
457(b) (government)	YES[3]	YES	NO	YES	YES	YES	YES	YES,[3,5] after 12/31/10
Qualified Plan [1] (pre-tax)	YES[3]	YES	NO	YES	YES[4]	YES	YES	YES,[3,5] after 9/27/10
403(b) (pre-tax)	YES[3]	YES	NO	YES	YES[4]	YES	YES	YES,[3,5] after 9/27/10
Designated Roth Account (401(k), 403(b) or 457(b)[2])	YES	NO	NO	NO	NO	NO	NO	Yes, if a direct trustee to trustee transfer

[1] Qualified plans include, for example, profit-sharing, 401(k), money purchase, and defined benefit plans
[2] Governmental 457(b) plans, after December 31, 2010
[3] Must include in income
[4] Must have separate accounts
[5] Must be an in-plan rollover
For more information regarding retirement plans and rollovers, visit Tax Information for Retirement Plans Community.

An Indirect Rollover to a Self-Directed IRA

An indirect rollover occurs when the IRA assets or qualified retirement plan assets are moved, first to the IRA holder or plan participant, before ultimately being sent to an IRA custodian.

60-Day Rollover Rule

An individual generally has sixty days from receipt of the eligible rollover distribution to roll the funds into an IRA. The 60-day period starts the day after the individual receives the distribution. Usually, no exceptions apply to the 60-day time period. In cases where the 60-day period expires on a Saturday, Sunday, or legal holiday, the individual may execute the rollover on the following business day. However, to avoid abuse of the rule, the Tax Code prescribes that taxpayers can only complete an IRA rollover once in a twelve-month period, which the IRS in the past has interpreted to apply to IRAs on an account-by-account basis. In turn, the "separate accounts" treatment of the IRA rollover rule potentially allows taxpayers to chain together multiple IRA rollovers, in an attempt circumvent the one-year rule and gain "temporary" use of IRA funds for an extended period of time. Even though IRS Publication 590 seems to suggest that the 60-day rule would apply to separate IRA accounts, many tax professionals have typically advised clients that the IRS could interpret the rule to apply to all IRAs because of the abuse of the 60-day distribution rule that could potentially occur.

Lo and behold, a recent Tax Court decision clarified how the IRS would interpret the 60-day rollover rule and whether it would apply to all IRAs or to separate IRAs. With the decision in *Bobrow v. Commissioner*, the IRS has shut down the separate-IRAs-rollover strategy altogether. In the aftermath of the *Bobrow* case, the IRS issued IRS Announcement 2014-15, stating that it will acquiesce to the Tax Court decision, update its Proposed Regulations and Publication 590, and issue new proposed regulations soon that will definitively apply the one-year IRA rollover rule on an IRA-aggregated basis going forward.

So what does all this mean? It is important to remember that this 60-day rule applies only to indirect rollovers; in other words, to funds that are not being transferred directly between retirement account custodians (i.e., financial institution, bank, trust company, and so forth). When funds are moved from retirement account to retirement account, that's considered a direct rollover or IRA transfer, and there is no 60-day limit or limit on the amount direct rollovers that can be done in a year.

In summary, as long as the funds are being moved from one retirement account to another, it can be done as many times as you would like. It's only when the retirement funds are sent to you individually that you have 60 days to re-contribute those funds to a retirement account. This can only be done once every twelve months, and any amounts not re-contributed would be subject to tax, as well as a 10 percent penalty if under the age of 59½.

"That is very helpful," Jen said. "When I left my prior employer, I moved the 401(k) plan funds to an IRA, which is where they are now. I was planning on doing a transfer of the IRA funds to a new self-directed IRA account."

"In general, regardless of which self-directed IRA custodian you work with, you will need to complete several self-directed IRA account application documents. The following is a summary of the primary documents you will need to complete," John surmised.

SELF-DIRECTED IRA ACCOUNT APPLICATION FORM

This form will help establish your self-directed IRA account with the IRA custodian you select. If you will be opening more than one IRA account—for example, a Roth IRA and an inherited IRA from a nonspouse—you need to complete a separate application form. In the account application, you need to designate the type of IRA you will be opening as well as your personal information. Also, the application typically includes language acknowledging the custodian's limited responsibilities, including the fact that the account will be a self-directed account and that the custodian has no fiduciary responsibilities. You will also include details on how you will be funding your self-directed IRA; for example, whether it is via a contribution, rollover, or transfer. In addition, you will need to include a photocopy of your driver's license.

EXPENSE PAYMENT REQUEST:

The purpose of this form is so the IRA custodian you select can pay an adviser in connection with the establishment of your self-directed IRA LLC structure. Since the self-directed IRA LLC setup involves your IRA and not you, your IRA should pay all IRA establishment fees. No personal funds should be used for the payment of any self-directed IRA establishment fees, including the LLC fee, as well as the IRA account setup fee. If you will not be using a checkbook control LLC, you will likely not need to complete the Expense Payment Request form.

REPRESENTATIVE AUTHORIZATION:

This form permits your tax adviser to contact the IRA custodian you select and discuss the status of your account (e.g., have they released your money to your LLC bank account) on your behalf. Note: This authorization can be rescinded by you at any time, and it will not need to provide your tax adviser with access to the IRA custodian account.

BENEFICIARY DESIGNATION:

This form allows you to designate a primary and contingent beneficiary for your IRA account in the case of your death. Note: Typically a spouse, if applicable, is designated as the primary beneficiary. In community property states, such as California, most custodians will require that a spouse be appointed as primary beneficiary of the account. To complete the Beneficiary of Designation Form:

- Include the name of the primary beneficiary and contingent beneficiary, if applicable; and
- Sign and date the Designation (spouse signature is also required if spouse is not designated as primary beneficiary)

IRA LLC AGREEMENT:

This form is used exclusively for those who wish to do a checkbook control self-directed IRA LLC structure. Because of the amount of freedom the structure offers the IRA holder, it is important for the IRA custodian to have some protection in case the IRA holder engages in an IRS-prohibited transaction. In other words, since the IRA account holder will be the manager of your IRA LLC, and will thus have checkbook control over investment of the assets, the IRA LLC Agreement Form serves as a form of defense for the custodian against the IRA client claiming a prohibited transaction was the responsibility of the custodian.

INTERNET ACCESS REQUEST:

This form allows you to check the status of your IRA services account online (i.e., to view funds).

TRANSFER AUTHORIZATION FORM:

This form is used by the new IRA custodian to request a transfer of your IRA funds from your current IRA custodian. For example, if your IRA is currently with Vanguard, the Transfer Authorization Form will be submitted to Vanguard by the new IRA custodian. The form will let your old IRA custodian (i.e., Vanguard) know that you wish to transfer your IRA funds to a new custodian and will provide Vanguard with all the transfer information. The IRA transfer is a direct custodian-to-custodian transfer, and there is no tax or penalty on the transfer. If you have non-IRA funds, such as a 401(k) plan or 403(b) funds, the Transfer Authorization Form is not required since, when it comes to non-IRA funds, you, as the plan participant, would need to initiate the rollover of the funds. You would likely need to contact the administrator of the plan and submit a document, which contains the information necessary to move the funds to the new IRA custodian. Typically, in order to get access to your non-IRA 401(k) funds for rollover purposes, your plan must allow for the rollover of the funds out of the plan. For most 401(k)-qualified retirement plans, there needs to be a triggering event, which allows the plan participant to gain access to the funds. In general, there are three main trigger events: (1) you leave your job with the company or agency that adopted the plan, (2) you reach the age of 59-1/2, or (3) the plan is terminated by the adopting employer. In Jen's case, she would generally not be able to rollover her 401(k) funds from her current employer since she is under 59-1/2 and will have no plan-triggering event; but she would be able to use her former employer retirement funds, which are now in an IRA, since she would not need to satisfy any 401(k) plan triggering rules and would be free, at her convenience, to transfer IRA assets tax-free by way of a direct transfer to a new IRA custodian.

INVESTMENT AUTHORIZATION:

This form authorizes the IRA custodian you have selected to release your IRA funds to your IRA investment, whether it is real estate or the funding of the checkbook LLC. Depending on the type of investments you will be making with the IRA, the custodian will likely require you to submit a set of documents for review. For example, for a checkbook IRA LLC investment, the IRA custodian would need to review copies of the LLC Articles of Organization, the LLC Tax Identification Number, and the LLC Operating Agreement. Whereas, a direct investment into real estate by the IRA custodian would require the submission of the following documents:

- Purchase Contract or Preliminary Settlement Statement in the name of IRA Financial Trust Company CFBO [Investor Name] [IRA Account No.]
- Estimated Closing Statement
- Preliminary Title Report
- Escrow documentation package, if applicable
- Nonrecourse Loan package, if applicable
- Proposed deed with "When Recorded Return To" IRA Financial Trust Company [ADDRESS]
- Recorded Grant Deed
- Title Insurance Policy

"Once the documents have been selected and reviewed by the IRA custodian, the custodian will execute the requisite documents and then end the IRA funds for investment. At that point, the self-directed IRA establishment process is complete. However, in the case of the checkbook control IRA LLC, there are several other items that need to be considered," John said.

"OK," Jen said. "I would like to hear about these items because I think I would consider the checkbook IRA."

"OK. Let's start talking with where you want to form your LLC. What state do you expect to buy real estate in at the outset?"

"I know I'll start off in Indiana," Jen said. "But I can see myself potentially doing investments in other states. Why is the state so important?" Jen asked

"Well, if you're buying real estate," John said, "I definitely recommend you form the LLC in the state where the real estate will be located to save on having to pay multiple filing fees. A state actually deems the LLC to be engaged in a trade or business if it owns property in that state. For example, if you own property in New York via an LLC, that state will deem you to be engaged in a trade or business and you would have to register the LLC with the state. If you formed the LLC in New York, that would not be an issue. But if you formed the LLC in another state, such as Delaware, then you would have to register your Delaware LLC as a foreign LLC in New York and pay New York fees. Then you could avail your LLC of the limited liability protection afforded by using an LLC. Taking this a step further, if you, for example, bought real estate in New York with a foreign LLC—let's say the LLC was formed in New Jersey—and there is a claim against the LLC, the plaintiff could try to argue that no limited liability protection exists because the LLC is not registered in New York and, thus, is not able to avail itself of the New York limited liability laws."

"So, the decision about where to form the LLC can have a financial impact on my IRA," Jen said.

"Exactly," John said. "For example, California imposes an $800 minimum franchise fee on every LLC doing business in the state. So, if you will not be buying real estate in California, then I would form the LLC in another state, such as Wyoming or Nevada. The residence of the IRA owner is not necessarily relevant to where the LLC should be formed because the LLC will be owned by the IRA and not the IRA holder. So, in your case, Mike, since you and Jen will be purchasing real estate with your IRA in Indiana, I would form your LLC in Indiana. That way you won't incur any additional LLC formation or annual fees."

"I have read a lot about people forming LLCs in Delaware, Nevada, and Wyoming," Jen said. "Should I think about this for my IRA?"

"In general," John began, "states such as Delaware, Nevada, and Wyoming are really popular for LLC formation purposes for a number of reasons. In the case of Delaware, the best reason for forming an LLC is that LLC laws there are considered well established. Experts think Delaware is very pro-company management. It also has a separate court system, the Court of Chancery, which is a court of equity and not a court of law.

"Amazing," Mike said, "that a state can have such a different tradition."

"Yes," John said. "Like Delaware, Nevada and Wyoming do not have state taxes and also share similar confidentiality characteristics. Now, if you were forming an entity that you would own personally or were looking to establish a fund that would attract foreign investors, then I would suggest considering Delaware. That's because the LLC will be owned by your IRA and not by you personally. IRAs, as I will explain, are protected from personal bankruptcy and in most states protected from creditor attack, so confidentiality is not as important. Also, IRAs don't pay income tax, so state tax exemption is also not as important as you might initially think."

"OK," Jen said, "that makes sense. So if I am buying real estate in Indiana, forming the LLC in Indiana is the most cost-effective approach. What if I was buying precious metals or just making hard-money loans?"

"In general, you should form the LLC in the state where the LLC will be conducting business or, in the case of an IRA, making the investment," John said. "Like real estate, if the business is being conducted in State A and you will be using an LLC, then the LLC must register to do business in State A. This isn't an issue if you form the LLC in State A. But if you form the LLC in State B, then the LLC must register as a foreign LLC in State A in order for it to avail itself of the limited liability protection in the state. So the question then becomes, What happens if the activity in the state does not rise to the level of a trade or business, such as buying stocks, holding precious metals, or making a loan? Well, if you were doing this activity personally, and not using IRA funds, then you could technically form the LLC in any state and then operate your investment activity as you see fit, since the state where you are operating will likely not deem that activity to be a trade or business."

"So you pay taxes where you do business regardless?" Jen asked.

"Exactly," John said. "From a state tax perspective, where you form your LLC for personal business purposes is not as relevant, because the state where you perform the activity will tax you on the income generated in the state. For example, if you operate an online business in New York—even if you have established a Delaware LLC for your business—because the income is being generated or sourced in New York, the State of New York will tax you on that income. Of course, you have to pay federal income tax on the income no matter where it is earned."

"So how does that all work for a self-directed IRA?" Jen asked.

"Since an IRA does not pay income tax," John said, "choosing the right state of formation depends on the type of activity being performed. As I said, real estate is treated as a business activity by most states. So, even though an IRA would not be subject to tax on income or gains generated by the real estate from a federal tax perspective, gaining limited liability protection for the asset would require you to form the LLC in the state where the real estate is located or to file an LLC that was formed in a different state as a foreign LLC in that state. Some people suggest always forming the LLC in a state such as Delaware or Nevada—and we talked about the reasons for this—but that would require you to incur dual state filing fees; the state filing fees from Delaware, for example, as well as the fees associated with establishing the LLC in the state where the real estate is located. Also, forming the LLC in a state such as Wyoming, with no state income tax, or a state such as Missouri, which has no LLC annual fees, will not allow you to circumvent any annual LLC franchise or state fees associated with the LLC where the real estate is located. So, if you established a self-directed IRA LLC in Missouri but bought property in California, you would be required to register the Missouri LLC to do business in California and would become subject to the California annual franchise fee. Again, because owning real estate by an LLC will deem the LLC to be treated as engaged in a trade or business in the state, even if your IRA will own the real estate and you consider it a passive asset, the states do not, and you will be required to register a foreign LLC to do business in that state if you want to avail yourself of the limited liability protection."

"What happens if I don't care about limited liability protection?" Jen asked. "Do I still have to register a foreign LLC in the state when I buy real estate?"

"Yes," John said. "Most likely, the title insurance company or attorney handling your real estate transaction will want to see paperwork showing that you are authorized to transact business in the state. So, even if you don't want to form the LLC in the state where you will be buying the real estate or register an LLC formed in another state as a foreign LLC in the state, you will likely be required to do so in any event in order to close on your real estate transaction."

"OK. I think it makes sense to form the IRA LLC in Indiana if I elected to go the checkbook IRA LLC route, since the real estate will be purchased in Indiana. What about a name for the LLC?" Jen asked.

"In general," John answered, "a self-directed IRA LLC may use any permissible name that is not the same as or deceivingly similar to existing corporations, partnerships, limited partnerships, or other LLCs. When forming your Self- Directed IRA LLC, the state will notify you whether the name you have selected is available. Some states, such as Utah, even make you reserve the name of your LLC before proceeding with the LLC formation process."

"Depending on the state statute," he continued, "certain words or abbreviations (e.g., "limited liability company," "L.L.C.") are generally required to be included in the name of the LLC. In selecting a name for your Self-Directed IRA LLC, be careful to include required language and avoid any prohibited language identified by the statute for the state in which the LLC is to be formed and the state in which the LLC is to operate. Some statutes prohibit the use of certain words in the name of the LLC that indicate or imply that the LLC is organized for a purpose other than the purpose stated in its Articles of Organization."

"In the case of a Self-Directed IRA LLC," he went on, "the question is often asked whether the name of the LLC must include the letters "IRA." The answer is no—there are no federal or state rules that specifically govern the creation of Self-Directed IRA LLCs. Accordingly, you are not required to include the letters "IRA" in the name of the Self-Directed IRA LLC, but you are permitted to do so. Most people tend to include the letters "IRA" in the name of their Self-Directed IRA LLC as a means of identifying the entity for investment purposes. However, a certain group of people would rather keep the identity of the owner of the LLC (the IRA) private. Therefore, it is also common for people to use generic names for naming their Self-Directed IRA LLC. For example, people will often use the street address of the investment property or other significant terms when naming their Self-Directed IRA LLC."

REGISTERED AGENT OF LLC AND ADDRESS OF LLC

"In general," John surmounted, "an LLC is required to have and maintain a registered agent and/or a registered office. A registered agent must be an individual residing in the state, a domestic corporation, or a foreign corporation authorized to do business in the state. The registered office is typically the business office of the registered agent. It need not be the same office as the LLC's business office. The purpose of a registered agent is to accept any process, notice, or demand required or permitted by law to be served upon the LLC. Anyone with an address in the state of formation can serve as LLC registered agent. In fact, there is an entire industry of companies that will serve as a registered agent for a fee.

"Makes sense," Jen said. "What about serving as manager of the LLC? Can I be the manager of the IRA LLC?" she asked.

"This is an important question," John admitted, "because the whole idea behind doing the self-directed IRA LLC checkbook control structure is to gain control over the IRA funds via the LLC, and the manager or managers are the person(s) authorized to control the operations and activities of the LLC as per the operating agreement. The *Swanson* case clearly states that an IRA holder may serve as manager, director, or officer of the newly established entity owned by his or her IRA without triggering a prohibited transaction.

"Would it be safer to have a third-party nondisqualified person serve as manager of the self-directed IRA LLC?" Jen asked.

"I know some IRA custodians who allow for checkbook control self-directed IRA LLC structures but require that the manager of the LLC be a nondisqualified person," John answered. "There does not seem to be any legal foundation for this argument, especially based on the *Swanson* case. Although, I guess it would be somewhat safer from an IRS-prohibited transaction standpoint to have a nondisqualified person serve as manager of the checkbook control IRA LLC. That said, I don't think it's necessary. Think about this: By granting a nondisqualified person discretion over all your LLC assets and investment decisions, you are essentially providing that person with 100 percent control over your hard-earned retirement funds. Now, sure, the person can be a sibling, friend, cousin, uncle, attorney, or CPA, but you had better trust that person like you trust yourself. For me, that's just too much faith to have in someone and it's potentially very risky."

"OK," Jen said. "Makes sense to me. But what happens in case I die? What happens to the LLC?"

"Whoever drafts your LLC Operating Agreement will hopefully include a provision that states that, upon your death, the LLC will be managed by your spouse or whoever you designate as the beneficiary of your IRA," John said. "It's important to nominate the successor manager in the case of your death to be the same person that you have appointed as your IRA beneficiary so that there is no conflict of interest. This way the IRA beneficiary and successor manager will be one and the same, can make LLC investment decisions that are aligned, and can also decide whether the IRA should be re-titled into the IRA beneficiary's name or not."

"Who is qualified to serve as IRA LLC manager?"

"With a self-directed IRA, the manager (IRA holder) keeps most of this power. He or she directs the investment, instead of a broker. Aside from life insurance, collectibles, and certain 'prohibited transaction' investments outlined in IRC Section 4975, a self-directed IRA can invest in most commonly made investments, including real estate, private business entities, public stocks, private stocks, and commercial paper."

"I definitely want to serve as manager of my self-directed IRA LLC," Jen said. "Can you give me an idea what of type of powers the manager would have?"

"Sure," John said. "The Self-Directed IRA LLC Operating Agreement describes the responsibilities and authority of the manager or the board of management. In most cases, the Self-Directed IRA LLC Operating Agreement will provide the manager with the authority to open a bank account on behalf of the LLC as well as have check-writing authority. In addition, the scope of any additional powers and responsibilities provided to the manager will be based on the contents of the Self-Directed IRA LLC Operating Agreement. For example, it is common for the manager to be given broad authority over the management and operations of the LLC since the member is an IRA, which is held in care of the IRA custodian. To this end, the manager of a self-directed IRA LLC is typically provided with the following powers and authority:

(i) to determine if additional capital contributions can be made,
(ii) whether to admit an additional member,
(iii) to determine the amount and timing of cash distributions to the members,
(iv) to determine the ability of the member to transfer its LLC interest to a third party,
(v) to determine the ability to appoint officers and directors,
(vi) to determine the ability to make investment decision on behalf of the LLC, which is known as checkbook control.

In addition, the manager will typically be appointed as the Tax Matters Partner (TMP) of the LLC. The purpose of a TMP is to provide a liaison between the LLC and the IRS during an administrative proceeding and to represent the LLC in judicial proceedings. As a result of the broad powers provided to the manager in connection with the self-directed IRA LLC structure," John continued, "including checkbook control, it's important that the self-directed IRA LLC Operating Agreement be drafted by an attorney with expertise in the area, so that the manager's responsibilities and powers are in line with IRS-prohibited transaction rules and IRS investment restrictions for an IRA. Since the manager in the self-directed IRA LLC structure will have the authority to make almost all LLC management decisions, including investment decisions, it's crucial that the Self-Directed IRA LLC Operating Agreement be drafted in a manner that includes the necessary prohibited transaction language to ensure that the investments made by the LLC will not violate IRS rules," John stated.

"I assume I cannot earn a few for serving as manager of the IRA LLC?" Jen asked.

"That is correct. No disqualified person can be compensated in any way for serving as manager of the LLC or providing any services," John said.

"Just to be clear," Jen said, "I would serve as the manager of the LLC but my IRA would be the member?"

"Correct," John said. "So to recap, in the case of an LLC, the manager(s) is the person or persons responsible for making all LLC-related decisions, including how LLC funds are being used and whether distributions will be made, whereas the member of the LLC is the owner of the LLC. In the case of a self-directed IRA LLC, the owner of the LLC would be the IRA. As we discussed, when completing the IRA custodian account setup paperwork, the Investment Authorization Form will allow the IRA custodian to transfer IRA funds to the LLC in return for ownership in the LLC. The IRA would be the owner of the LLC. This means that all profits, losses, and income attributable to the IRA LLC will be allocated to the IRA as owner/member and not the manager. The manager does not have any economic interest in the LLC; he or she makes decisions on behalf of the LLC, but does not share in any of the income or gains."

"So just to be clear," Jen said, "when the IRA LLC makes investments, I don't report the income or losses on my personal income tax return?"

"That's right," John said. "Remember, the LLC is owned by an IRA and not you. An IRA is treated as a tax-exempt trust pursuant to IRC Section 408 (IRC Section 408A in the case of a Roth IRA) and, as a result, does not file any income tax returns. Since you do not own any of the LLC and are just the manager, none of the income, gains, or losses from the IRA LLC will be reported by you on your personal income tax return (IRS Form 1040). Just like if you used you IRA funds to buy Apple or Google stock and you generated gains, the income would just flow back to your IRA, and the gains would not be reported on your income tax return. The IRS would know whether your IRA gained in value from the IRS Form 5498 that the IRA custodian is required to file each year, but this would not be reported on your personal income tax return because you would not be the owner of the IRA LLC. Really the only time you would report any IRA activity on your personal income tax return is when you took an IRA distribution."

"So how do I show LLC ownership?" Jen asked.

"The LLC that I will help you establish," said John, "which will ultimately be owned by your IRA, will be newly established and, until IRA funds have been transferred to the LLC and the Operating Agreement signed, will be just a shell company with no ownership. The ownership of the LLC will be documented by the LLC Operating Agreement, which will show the amount invested by the IRA member and the related ownership. As a result, the transfer of the IRA funds to the new LLC will begin the process of funding the LLC. The capital contribution table, typically shown on an LLC Operating Agreement Exhibit at the end of the agreement, will show the member's name and the corresponding value of the cash or asset contributed, along with the percentage of ownership. In the case of an LLC owned by one IRA, which is referred to as a single-member LLC or a disregarded entity for tax purposes, the ownership is always 100 percent."

"That's very helpful," Mike said. "And it brings to mind a few questions."

"Fire away," John enthused.

"We will likely be using Jen's IRA initially, but I also have a small IRA with a brokerage firm. Can I also use those funds if we did a self-directed IRA LLC?"

"That's a good question," John said. "You can rollover any type of retirement account into a self-directed IRA structure. In your case, you and Jen would each need to open separate IRA accounts with the IRA custodian, and then your IRAs can both fund the LLC. The LLC would then have two owners, and the LLC would be considered a partnership for income tax purposes. There would be no partnership level tax that would be due, but a partnership return would be required to be filed."

"I get it," Mike said. "Is there an advantage to having a single-member LLC versus a partnership?"

"Generally, it's to your advantage to have an LLC that is treated as a disregarded entity for tax purposes, because a disregarded entity is not required to file a federal income tax return. For many people, this is important because not having to file a partnership tax return is certainly easier and less costly than having to hire a CPA and a tax preparer, or use an online filing source to file the partnership tax return. Also, some people believe that the less paperwork that is filed with the IRS the better. As long as you will not be engaged in a prohibited transaction, there is nothing to be worried about when it comes to filing a return. And not having to file a return is certainly much easier and requires no cost."

"Can a self-directed IRA LLC be owned by multiple IRAs?" Jen asked.

"In the *Swanson* case, Mr. Swanson's IRA was the sole member of the newly established entity and, thus, was the only retirement account that purchased stock in the entity. As a result, it is quite clear that an IRA can own a wholly owned interest in a newly established entity. However, based on the *Swanson* case and the IRS Field Service Advisory Memorandum, a number of attorneys as well as IRA custodians have taken the position that more than one IRA, including traditional and Roth IRAs as well as IRAs belonging to family members, can become owners of a newly established entity, as long as the IRA funds were invested *simultaneously* into the new entity. The thinking behind this position follows the Tax Court's holding in *Swanson* that a new corporation without shares doesn't fit within the definition of a disqualified person under the prohibited transaction rules. Accordingly, only after one or more IRAs purchased an interest in the newly established entity would be the entity become disqualified. In addition, since the only benefit the IRA holders would experience from investment in the new entity would be one they would be entitled to as beneficiary of the IRA, which is exempted from the prohibited transaction rules pursuant to IRC Section 4975(d)(9), the belief is that an investment by or one more IRAs into a newly established entity would not trigger a prohibited transaction."

"So how would profits and losses be allocated?" Jen asked.

"Great question," John asked. "Computing the amount of LLC profits or losses is important in determining the amount of profits or losses that should flow through to IRA members. In the case of an LLC owned by one member, the determination of the percentage of profits and losses allocated to the member is always 100 percent. However, when there are two or more members of an LLC, the determination of the amount of profits and losses allocated to each member is typically based on the economic arrangement between the members and is generally documented in the members' agreement or LLC Operating Agreement. The LLC Operating Agreement is the core document that will identify how profits, losses, and cash will be allocated or distributed to the members. The LLC Operating Agreement is also crucial for any LLC that will have more than one member."

"How does it usually work?" Jen asked.

"Typically, the profits and losses of an LLC are allocated based on the amount of cash contributed by the members to the LLC," John said. "For example, if John and Steve each contribute $1,000 to the LLC, they will typically each be provided a 50 percent interest in the profits, losses, and cash distributions of the LLC. This means that they each will be allocated 50 percent of the LLC profits or losses in a year. So, if John and Steve's LLC generated $1,000 in profits in year one, they would each be allocated $500 of profits. In some cases, a member may receive an interest in the LLC for the performance of services (a profits interest) without contributing any cash to the LLC; in others, the members may have a more complex financial arrangement. But, in the case of a self-directed IRA LLC, the members' (IRA) ownership interest is typically based on the amount of IRA funds invested in the LLC."

"So even though the IRA will own the LLC," Jen surmised, "the LLC will still operate like a typical for-profit LLC?"

"Right," John said. "Therefore, the manager of the LLC will have the authority to open a regular business checking account for the LLC at any local bank or trust company. The LLC can also open a savings account, but in most cases involving a self-directed IRA LLC, a checking account will be required so that investments can be made using IRA funds. Just remember that, when you're opening the LLC bank account, you want to open an LLC business checking account, not an IRA account. You'll already have an IRA account with the IRA passive custodian, so you won't need to open a new IRA. Each bank has its own internal rules concerning the documents you need to possess in order to open an LLC business checking account. The majority of banks and trust companies will require the following documents:

LLC Articles of Organization

"The LLC Articles of Organization are very similar to a corporation's Certificate of Formation. The LLC Articles of Organization is the document that establishes the LLC pursuant to state statute as well as identifying the name of the LLC, the LLC address, and the name of the registered agent. Before opening an LLC bank account, the majority of banks will require a copy of the LLC Articles of Organization and/or the LLC Certificate of Formation to ensure that the LLC is valid and has been established," John said.

The LLC Tax Identification Number/ Employer Identification Number

"The LLC Tax Identification Number/Employer Identification Number ("EIN") is used to identify and collect information about the LLC. The EIN is comparable to the way a Social Security number is assigned to all US citizens. Most businesses are required to acquire an EIN for purposes of opening a business bank account. In the case of a self-directed IRA LLC, an EIN would be required to be obtained in order to open the LLC bank checking account since the IRA holder is not the owner of the LLC, but just the manager. As your tax adviser, I would acquire a tax ID number for your IRA LLC from the IRS," John stated.

LLC Operating Agreement

In some cases, the bank may request a copy of the Self-Directed IRA LLC Operating Agreement. The LLC Operating Agreement is the core document, referred to when issues concerning the self-directed IRA LLC need to be resolved. In addition, the LLC Operating Agreement is the document that identifies the member(s) and manager(s) of the LLC—which is especially important in the case of a self-directed IRA. Remember, with a self-directed IRA LLC, the IRA holder is not a member/owner of the LLC, but is typically just the manager. In other words, the IRA holder does not have any economic or financial interest in the LLC, but is simply serving as the manager of the LLC. A properly drafted Self-Directed IRA LLC Operating Agreement will explicitly set forth the responsibilities and activities of the manager, which typically include the ability to open a bank account on behalf of the LLC as well as have check-writing authority over the LLC bank account."

"So opening a bank account for a self-directed IRA LLC is a lot like opening a standard LLC bank account. The only difference is that, in the case of a standard LLC, typically the manager is also a member of the LLC and, in the case of a self-directed IRA LLC, the manager—the IRA holder—is not a member of the LLC," Jen stated.

"Yes—you are 100 percent correct," John smiled.

"That is really helpful. I understand that if I elected to use a custodian-controlled self-directed IRA account, the custodian would be a lot more involved in the investment process versus a checkbook IRA. However, if I elected to use a checkbook IRA LLC, what exactly would the IRA custodian be doing each year? Jen asked.

"With a self-directed IRA LLC with checkbook control," John began, "all IRA investments are made via the LLC without custodian consent. This means that once the IRA custodian has invested the IRA holder's IRA funds into the new LLC, the LLC manager and not the IRA custodian becomes the party responsible for making and executing IRA investments. Accordingly, when an IRA investment is made, it will be made at the LLC level. In other words, the LLC manager, not the IRA custodian, will be the party that makes the IRA investment determination. As a result, the IRA custodian will have no involvement in the investment.

John continued his explanation. "Starting in 2015 and beyond, the IRS updated the IRS Form 5498 to include new Boxes 15a and 15b. The fair market value of investments in the IRA will be reported in Box 15a. Box 15b will be used to categorize the types of investments listed in Box 15a through the use of category code(s). Check you inbox for what the category codes will look like."

John sent Mike and Jen an e-mail that included the following document:

A - Stock or other ownership interest in a corporation that is not readily tradable on an established US or foreign securities market.

B Short- or long-term debt obligation that is not traded on an established securities market.

C - Ownership interest in a limited liability company or similar entity (unless the entity is traded on an established securities market).

D - Real estate.

E - Ownership interest in a partnership, trust, or similar entity (unless the entity is traded on an established securities market).

F - Option contract or similar product that is not offered for trade on an established US or foreign option exchange.

G - Other asset that does not have a readily available fair market value.

H - More than two types of assets (listed in A through G) that are held in the IRA.

"Is that a big difference from previous years?" Jen asked.

"Somewhat," John answered. "The reporting change seems to signal an interest on behalf of the IRS to get a better handle on the type of IRA assets that are being purchased with IRA funds and get a better handle on what percentage of IRA assets should be considered 'hard-to-value' assets."

"Interesting," Jen said. "Does this new change mean that the IRS may be looking to start auditing IRAs more frequently?"

"It's hard to say," John said. "It seems clear that the IRS is trying to get a better handle on the amount of IRA assets that are being invested in alternative assets. I don't think this is a means for the IRS to try to find out whether an IRA is engaged in a prohibited transaction, but is more about its concern that certain IRA assets' fair market values are not being reported accurately. The fair market value of an IRA asset is very important to the IRS because that is what a tax would be imposed on. I don't think this is going to trigger an IRS witch hunt for self-directed IRA accounts, but it's clear that the IRS feels that certain IRA assets are not being valued accurately."

"So as long as I'm playing straight, I'll be fine. Same as any other IRS matter."

"Yes. And as far as immediate concerns go, there's nothing to worry about with respect to the new IRS Form 5498 requirements if you are not engaging in any transaction that violates the IRS prohibited transaction rules," John said.

"Does the IRA custodian do anything other than filing the IRS Form 5498?" Jen asked.

"Essentially," John responded, "the IRA custodian is responsible for the following:

- Assisting in opening and funding your IRA account
- Making investment(s) on your behalf
- Making distributions and paying expenses per your request
- Providing you with quarterly statements
- Answering questions about your account and our procedures

- Reporting information required by the IRS and other governmental agencies
  - IRS Form 1099R—Distributions from your IRA
  - IRS Form 5498—Contributions to, and Fair Market Value of, your IRA

Also, keep in mind that an IRA custodian is not permitted to give investment, legal, or tax advice," John added.

"I get it," Jen said. "The IRA custodian is simply a conduit that allows me to make IRA investments. It is not a fiduciary and does not offer any investment advice or sell financial investment products. It will only make IRA investments at the sole direction of the IRA holder."

"Yes—that is pretty much it," John said.

"And if I elect to use a checkbook control IRA LLC, once my IRA funds have been sent to the LLC I am free to start making investments with my self-directed IRA LLC," Jen noted.

"You sure are," John said. "As the manager of the self-directed IRA LLC, you will have the freedom to make all investment decisions for your self-directed IRA LLC. In other words, you will have checkbook control over your IRA funds, allowing you to make an IRA investment by simply writing a check or wiring funds directly from the IRA LLC bank account."

"I like the sound of that."

"You should. And since your IRA will become the owner(s)/(member(s)) of the newly formed IRA LLC, all income and gains generated by an IRA LLC investment will generally flow back to your IRA tax-free. Because an LLC is treated as a pass-through entity for federal income tax purposes, all income and gains are taxed at the owner level, not the entity level. However, since an IRA is a tax-exempt party pursuant to IRC Section 408 and, thus, does not pay federal income tax, all IRA LLC investment income and gains will generally flow through to the IRA tax-free!"

"Even better," Jen said. "Thanks for this explanation. It was thorough but critical."

"Before we get off the call, I just wanted to offer some helpful tips I have shared with my clients for making self-directed IRA investments," John submitted.

"That would be valuable," Jen replied.

"Whether you decide to establish a custodian-controlled self-directed IRA or a checkbook control IRA, a handful of tips are useful to keep in mind when making investments with a self-directed IRA.

1. Make sure you perform adequate diligence on the property you will be purchasing, especially if it is in a state you do not live in.
2. Whether you are purchasing real estate or making any investment with your IRA, make sure to use only retirement funds and that no personal funds, from you or any disqualified person, are being used. For example, on a real estate purchase, the deposit and purchase price for the real estate property should be paid using self-directed IRA funds or funds from a nondisqualified third party.
3. Remember those prohibited transaction rules we discussed in depth; it's important to remember that no personal funds or funds from a "disqualified person" should be used.
4. In connection with the IRA investment, all expenses, repairs, taxes, expenditures, or related fees should be paid using retirement funds— no personal funds should be used.
5. If additional funds are required for improvements or other matters involving the IRA investments, all funds should come from the self-directed IRA or from a "nondisqualified person."
6. No services in connection with the retirement-account investment should be performed by the IRA holder or any "disqualified person.". In general, no active services, only necessary and required tasks, in connection with the maintenance of the self-directed IRA structure should be performed by the IRA holder or any "disqualified person" with respect to the IRA transaction.
7. All income, gains, or losses from the self-directed IRA investment should be allocated to the IRA or IRA LLC if a checkbook control IRA structure is used.

8. Title to the real estate or asset purchased should be in the name of the self-directed IRA. For example, if Joe Smith established a self-directed IRA LLC and named the LLC XYZ, LLC, title to real estate purchased by Joe's self-directed IRA LLC would be as follows: XYZ LLC. Alternatively, if Jim established a self-directed IRA with ABC Trust Company, the investment would be titled as follows: ABC Trust Company, CFBO Jim Smith IRA.

9. For a real estate transaction, if financing is needed, remember that only nonrecourse financing should be used. A nonrecourse loan is a loan that is not personally guaranteed and whereby the lender's only recourse is against the property and not against the borrower.

10. Take into account the UBTI tax rules, which could be triggered in one of the following ways: (i) using a nonrecourse loan to purchase real estate, (ii) using margin to buy stock, and (iii) the purchase of a trade or business operated through a flow-through entity, such as an LLC.

11. The UBTI tax rates can run as high as 40 percent, so it is important to take into account the rules and how they could potentially impact your IRA investment.

12. Keep good records of income and expenses generated by the self-directed IRA investment, especially with a checkbook control IRA. The bank account statements and transaction documentation is generally sufficient to show the flow of funds with respect to the investment.

13. Make sure to perform adequate diligence on the IRA investment, especially if you will be investing with third-party promoters or purchasing assets in a state you do not live in."

"That was extremely helpful," Jen said.

"One more thing I wanted to mention is beware of fraud, especially if you will be investing with third-party promoters. While self-directed IRAs and 401(k) plans can be a safe way to invest retirement funds, investors should be mindful of potential fraudulent schemes when using a self-directed retirement structure."

"Any examples?" Mike requested.

"Recently," John offered, "the Securities and Exchange Commission ("SEC") issued an Investor Alert to warn investors of the potential risks of fraud associated with investing through Self-Directed Individual Retirement Accounts (self-directed IRAs and solo 401(k) plans). The SEC notes that there has been an increase in reports or complaints of fraudulent investment schemes that utilized a self-directed IRA or solo 401(k) plan as a key feature."

"So what do you watch out for?" Mike asked.

"You always need to undertake your own evaluation of the merits of any proposal, and you should check with regulators about the background and history of an investment and its promoters before making a decision when considering a self-directed retirement structure. You should understand that the custodians of a self-directed retirement account may have limited duties to investors, and that the custodians and trustees for these accounts will generally not evaluate the quality or legitimacy of an investment and its promoters. As with every investment, investors also need to undertake their own evaluation of the merits of a proposal, and they should check with regulators about the background and history of an investment and its promoters before making a decision," John said.

John mentioned to Mike that he just e-mailed him a list of some helpful information and links to a number of organizations that can help a retirement investor better protect his or her retirement assets from fraud.

- SEC: The SEC provides information on different products, asset allocations, and risk. http://www.sec.gov/investor/seniors.shtml
- FINRA: FINRA provides an online service called Broker Check for investors to check the backgrounds of brokers. http://www.finra.org/Investors/ToolsCalculators/BrokerCheck/
- FINRA's website also has tools and resources to protect senior investors and help them make informed investment decisions, including "Investor Alerts" that provide timely information on steering clear of investment scams and problems. See http://www.finra.org/Investors/ProtectYourself/InvestorAlerts/index.htm.

- NASAA: The North American Securities Administrators Association (NASAA) also has helpful information available for specific states. This organization is very proactive in providing resources for senior investors. http://www.nasaa.org/investor-education/
- FTC: The Federal Trade Commission (FTC) works for the consumer to prevent fraudulent, deceptive, and unfair business practices in the marketplace and to provide information to help consumers spot, stop, and avoid them. It also enters Internet, telemarketing, identity theft, and other fraud-related complaints into Consumer Sentinel, a secure online database available to hundreds of civil and criminal law enforcement agencies in the United States and abroad. The FTC website is http://www.ftc.gov, or call 877-FTC-HELP.
- BBB: The Better Business Bureau (BBB), www.BBB.org, is also an excellent resource for researching businesses that have been reported for fraudulent or deceptive practices.
- AARP: The American Association of Retired Persons (AARP) has provided resources and funding for many research projects in various states in order to uncover scams targeted at senior citizens. It also has numerous free publications to help seniors become more astute investors. Go to http://www.aarp.org.

John also attached to the e-mail another list, which covered some helpful tips that will help avoid fraudulent investments and prevent Mike and Jen from being financially cheated, to wit:

- Shred financial documents and paperwork with personal information before you discard them.
- Protect your Social Security number. Give it out only if absolutely necessary or ask to use another identifier.
- Don't give out personal information over the phone, mail, or the Internet unless you know who you are dealing with.
- Don't give out passwords for any of your accounts to anyone.
- Don't give out your credit card numbers to any strangers.

- If you believe the contact is legitimate, go to the company's website by typing in the site address directly or using a page you have previously bookmarked, instead of using a link provided in an e-mail.
- Be aware of being kept on the phone for a long time.
- Be wary of promises of quick profits, offers to share "inside" information, and pressure to invest before you have an opportunity to investigate.
- Words like "guarantee," "high return," "limited offer," or "as safe as a CD" are red flags.
- Watch out for offshore scams and investment "opportunities" in other countries.
- Watch out if a company is not registered with the SEC or the secretary of state where it is located.
- Be cautious if a financial adviser cannot be found through FINRA.
- Ask the online promoter whether—and how much—he or she is being paid to sell the product.
- Make sure you understand the investment before you invest your money.
- Take your time to make decisions.
- Be sure to talk over all financial decisions with a trusted family member, friend, or financial adviser.
- Report any actual frauds and any potential investment frauds affecting Americans to local, state, or federal regulators.
- Never make a check out to a financial adviser.
- Never allow statements or confirmations to be sent directly to your financial adviser without receiving copies.
- Pressure to trade the account in a manner that is inconsistent with your investment goals and the risk you want or can afford to take.

"In general," John added, "the best prevention technique is to identify and research the persons, products, and companies offering their services. The more education and understanding of the product features, especially investment products, the higher the level of scrutiny you can apply. In the event of any suspicious calls, e-mails, or personal solicitations, you should report them to the proper authorities."

"Got it," Mike said.

"Always take the time you need to understand and evaluate a potential investment. Make sure you understand the investment you will be making and thoroughly understand how the promoter will be able to generate the returns being promised. Also, make sure the promoter of the investment has the necessary qualifications or licenses, if applicable, to offer the investment. Be cautious if a sponsor or adviser uses the affiliation as the reason to make the investment, rather than relying on the underlying merits of the investment or trust in the salesperson."

"Sounds good," Mike agreed.

KEEPING YOUR SELF-DIRECTED IRA LLC IN GOOD STANDING

"If you elect to do a checkbook control IRA, then you will also need to make sure you meet your LLC tax return filing requirements. Whereas, if you use the custodian-controlled self-directed IRA to make a real estate investment, for example, then no LLC filing requirements would be required," John said.

"How do I do that?" Mike asked.

"If your self-directed IRA LLC is owned by one IRA, the LLC is treated as a disregarded entity for federal income tax purposes. So no federal income tax return is required to be filed. But, if your LLC is owned by two or more IRAs, the LLC is treated as a partnership for tax purposes and a federal partnership tax return (IRS Form 1065) and a state return must be filed. You should consult a tax professional for more information to determine whether your self-directed IRA LLC may have any federal or state income tax filing requirements."

"What about annual LLC fees?" Jen asked.

"Some states require annual reports and impose an annual fee for every LLC that was formed in the state," John said. "The state should notify you of this, however. John jotted down a web page for Mike and Jen, which provides a summary of the LLC annual fees per state. - http://www.irafinancialgroup. com/llc-formation-fees.php. You should consult a tax professional for more information on what annual fees, if any, may apply to your self-directed IRA LLC."

IRA VALUATION

"Finally," John said, "you need to report the valuation of the self-directed IRA each year, including the value of the investments and any cash. Your IRA custodian will send you a form at the end of each year requesting that you provide a valuation of your IRA LLC. The valuation will then be submitted by the IRA custodian to the IRS on Form 5498, which every custodian by law is required to complete. You should consult a tax professional for assistance."

"Will do," Mike said. "That's helpful."

"All in all," John said, "unlike what many financial advisers will tell you, using a Self-Directed IRA is quite easy and stress-free. However, a number of items exist that you should be careful about when making an investment with a Self-Directed IRA. Working with a Self-Directed IRA facilitation firm or consulting with a tax professional is highly advisable."

"I'll make sure to do that," Jen said.

CONCLUSION

THE PRIMARY OBJECTIVE of this book is to reveal the exciting benefits that the Self-Directed IRA can offer you from a retirement, tax, and investment perspective, and demonstrate how easy and simple it is to establish and operate. My goal is to have you, the reader, learn in a nutshell all the key points to establishing and operating a self-directed IRA. I use the characters of Mike, Jen, and John to illustrate the kind of dialogue I have experienced talking with over 15,000 retirement investors, exploring the ins and outs of the Self-Directed IRA. Mike, Jen, and John and the fictitious questions and answers they exchange are designed to give you a sense of the types of issues and matters that you need to consider when (1) establishing a Self-Directed IRA, (2) contributing to a Self-Directed IRA, (3) making Self-Directed IRA investments, and, ultimately (4) taking distributions from the IRA.

Jen and Mike represent the typical Self-Directed IRA investors who are interested in using a self-directed IRA to invest in real estate or in other alternative asset investments. The questions Jen and Mike pose to John are typical of the questions someone looking at the Self-Directed IRA would ask a tax professional. It is my hope that, by using this type of dialogue format, the book will address the Self-Directed IRA structure, while still being engaging and interesting.

I hope that I've helped you understand the different types of Self-Directed IRA options that are available to you and some of their advantages and disadvantages. Most importantly, I hope the book has been able to show you the enormous benefits of having and growing a retirement account and some of the ways you can accomplish this, all of which are simple and easy. Whether you have a pretax traditional IRA or an after-tax Roth IRA, or convert from a pretax IRA to a Roth IRA, taking the time to focus on growing your IRA through contributions and investments will be the difference between retiring rich and working the rest of your life.

Unlike what some financial advisers or planners may lead to you to think, using a self-directed IRA is 100 percent legal; in fact it even says so right on the IRS website, and it is easy and quite inexpensive. I hope the book has shown you that, so long as you do not purchase collectibles or life insurance, or engage in a prohibited transaction such as buying a house and living in it, you don't have much to worry about when it comes to the IRS. Like traditional investments, such as stocks and mutual funds, the self-directed IRA industry has, over the last several years, seen a reduction in annual IRA custodian fees, which now can be as low as just a few hundred dollars a year.

This book is not about how you should invest your retirement funds, which is a conversation best left for you to have with your investment adviser or financial planner. However, I hope the book has shown you that investing in real estate or other alternative assets is legal and can be done quite easily and inexpensively with a self-directed IRA.

I am sure that many of you are probably wondering why this is the first book you've read on how much personal control and influence you can have on your retirement funds. People ask me, "How can that be?" They think that it sounds almost seems too good to be true.

Don't blame yourself for not knowing. You are not alone. I have talked to tens of thousands of retirement account holders, and I am always amazed at how few people realize you can buy real estate or make other nontraditional assets with retirement money. I understand how they feel. I have a law degree and a masters in taxation and have worked at some of the largest law firms in the world. While I am hardly the most sophisticated investor, I have a diverse tax and investment background. But I only learned about alternative investment options through the research I did for a client.

Since then, I've helped a number of tax partners I used to work with, one of whom even went to Yale Law School, who were unaware that retirement assets can be invested outside of traditional financial markets.

I can't stress it enough. This is what the major financial institutions want. The increasingly huge retirement investment world is a $25 trillion industry with billions of potential fees. Many Americans are cash poor but retirement rich, and these financial institutions are counting on the fees from those accounts to bolster their bottom lines.

Using retirement funds to make alternative asset investments is not for everyone. That said, the goal of this book is to illustrate how buying real estate or making other alternative assets with retirement funds through a Self-Directed IRA is an option that does not have to be scary or expensive. In fact, it is quickly becoming an option more and more people are starting to consider. According to the data provider Preqin, the alternative assets industry added more than $600 billion in assets under management in 2013 and, as of January 2015, consists of some $6 trillion in assets. These numbers are even more impressive when you consider that the alternative asset investment market is not overly advertised to the average American, especially when it comes to retirement accounts. When was the last time you saw a TV commercial from a major bank proclaiming an opportunity to buy real estate or gold through your IRA? Those institutions do not allow their IRA accounts to invest in any alternative asset class for the simple reason that they don't make money when you purchase real estate or other alternative assets. But they do make money when you buy their financial products. The genie is now out of the bottle and more and more American retirement investors are starting to learn about the Self-Directed IRA and some of the exciting retirement, tax, and investment benefits it presents.

I hope the book is able to show you, without too much unnecessary detail, that using a self-directed IRA can be easy, fun, and cost-effective, as well as offer your retirement account the potential for asset diversification, inflation protection, asset growth, tax-free investing, asset protection, and estate planning opportunities. Yes, there are rules to follow, such as the prohibited transaction rules, and there is the potential for fraud from shady investment promoters. But if you work with a qualified Self-Directed IRA facilitation company, tax attorney, or CPA, having a Self-Directed IRA can be easy, stress-free, economical, and fun, and can allow you to invest tax-free in what you know and understand.

Made in the USA
Columbia, SC
21 February 2021

33359288R00098